Hearts Have Changed

Stories of the Sahabah
Volume IV

Adapted by
Noura Durkee

IQRA'
International Educational Foundation
Chicago

Part of IQRA's Comprehensive and Systematic Program of Islamic Studies

Stories of the Sahabah: Volume IV
Hearts Have Changed

Program of Social Studies
Junior Level/General

Chief Program Editors
Dr. Abidullah al-Ansari Ghazi
Ph.D., Comparative Religions
Harvard University

Tasneema Khatoon Ghazi
Ph.D., Curriculum-Reading
University of Minnesota

Copyright © June 2000, IQRA' International
Educational Foundation. All Rights Reserved.

First printing, Cedar Graphics, USA

IQRA' International Educational Foundation,
7450 Skokie Blvd., Skokie, IL 60077
Tel: 847-673-4072; Fax: 847-673-4095
E-mail: iqra@aol.com
Website: http://www.iqra.org

Religious Review
Imam Abdool Rahman Khan
B.A., University of Madinah

Translators
Dr. Muhammad Fadel
Ph.D., University of Chicago

Maulana Abdur-Rahman
Sayeed Siddiqui

Dr. Iman al-Gorab
University of Alexandria

Editors
Elkheir Elkheir
M.A., University of Wisc-Madison
M.A., University of Leeds, England

Fareeha Khan
B.S., B.A. Loyola University Chicago

Huseyin Abiva
M.A., University of Maryland

Designers
Michelle Haynes
School of the Art Inst. of Chicago

'Isa Muhammad ibn Colone
B.A., B.S., University of Puerto Rico

Cover Illustration
Sharon K. Jaman
Carnegie-Mellon University

Macros Design
Muhammad Zakariya

Library of Congress Control Number 99-080153
ISBN 1-56316-453-1

الله أكبر

Table of Contents

✦

*This volume is dedicated to
the late Maulana Abdur Rahman Sayeed
Siddiqui, an enthusiastic
supporter of IQRA's vision.
His personality symbolized
the best of Islamic values.
May his soul rest in the Mercy of Allah* ﷻ.

IQRA's Note

*I*QRA' International Educational Foundation is pleased to offer *Hearts Have Changed*, the fourth volume in the series *Stories of the Sahabah*. Adapted by Noura Durkee, this volume contains the biographies of seventeen *Sahabah* of Rasūlullāh ﷺ who testified to the truth of Islam after their hearts were opened by the mercy of Allah ﷻ. In this volume, you will read about the lives of several of the *Sahabah*--their lives before Islam, the circumstances surrounding their acceptance of Islam, and how they lived their lives on the path of Allah ﷻ thereafter. When describing his *Sahabah*, Rasūlullāh ﷺ remarked: "The best generation is that of mine; then those who will follow." (*Sahīh Muslim* 6: 159) He ﷺ also said: "Do not abuse my companions, for if any one of you spend gold equal to Uhud (in the Cause of Allah ﷻ), it would not be equal to a portion or even a half a portion spent by one of them." (*Sahīh al-Bukhari* 5:22) Rasūlullāh ﷺ continued to extol the virtues of his *Sahābah* throughout his life.

These *Saḥābah* ﷺ stood firmly with Rasūlullāh ﷺ through all his ordeals, never abandoning him in the face of adversity. They gave up their families, their homes and their worldly possessions to safeguard the Messenger ﷺ and his message. They emulated their beloved Prophet ﷺ and followed his ways and instructions (*Sunnah*) as closely as humanly possible, preserving the teachings of the Qur'an and the *Sunnah* during his life and continuing their preservation after his death.

Among all the prophets and saintly figures of the distant past, that shining beacon of guidance, Muhammad ﷺ, is the only person whose life, teachings, and actions have been accurately recorded and preserved. His life is free from the myths and legends that have so often plagued the figures of other much older religious traditions. The example of the *Saḥābah* and their determination to reflect the moral lifestyle of Rasūlullāh ﷺ has continued to guide millions of Muslims throughout the world.

The Stories of the Saḥābah series presents the lives of the *Saḥābah* for both younger generations of Muslims and the general public and offers the biographies of these role models who are only next to the Messenger ﷺ in their importance in Islam. The biographies have been adapted by Noura Durkee from Arabic and Urdu sources in translation, and she has been able to convey these stories in an engaging and comprehensive way.

Additional useful features of the book include an appendix, which consists of a list of the transliterated names of the *Saḥābah* and historical figures, along with a glossary of terms, the IQRA' Transliteration Chart and definitions of the Islamic invocations used as a standard throughout all IQRA' publications.

May Allah ﷻ reward all the authors whose works we have referenced: Abd ur-Rahman Basha, *Suwar min Ḥayāt as-Saḥābah*; Muḥammad ad-Dawlah, *Qaṣaṣ min Ḥayāt as-Saḥābah*; Khalid Muhammad Khalid, *Rijāl Ḥawla Rasūlullāh*; and Talib Hashmi, *Rasulullah ke Chalis Jan-nisar*.

To the readers of this book, we ask that you remember all of us in your *Du'a'* and continue to support IQRA's educational mission as it belongs to you, the *Ummah* of the Seal of the Prophets and Messengers, Aḥmad Muhammad Muṣtafā ﷺ.

Chief Editors
IQRA' International
Educational Foundation

Abu Hurairah ad-Dawsi al-Yamani

*"O Allah... I ask you for knowledge
that is never forgotten."*
Abu Hurairah

Abu Hurairah ﷺ is one of the best known of all the *Sahabah*. He was from the tribe of Daws which lived deep in the desert. He was known in those days as 'Abd ash-Shams, the "Servant of the Sun." While living among his people, he heard about Islam and became a Muslim at the hands of his friend at-Tufail ibn 'Amr ad-Dawsi ﷺ. The two remained with their people, trying to bring them to the way of Allah ﷻ. Because of this mission, 'Abd ash-Shams ﷺ didn't come to Madinah until six years

1

after the *Hijrah*. And when he finally did, 'Abd ash-Shams came with a large group of his tribe. They had left all their belongings behind. 'Abd ash-Shams kept nothing of his material goods and relied solely on his faith. In Madinah, 'Abd ash-Shams ﷺ lived with the *Ahl-as-Suffah*, "the People of the Bench." These were very poor men who had been given a place to stay within the *masjid* of Rasulullah ﷺ itself.

'Abd ash-Shams loved Madinah and was very eager to meet the Blessed Prophet ﷺ. When he first met Rasulullah ﷺ, the Prophet ﷺ asked him, "What's your name?"

"'Abd ash-Shams," he replied.

"It is better to be 'Abd ar-Rahman, the Servant of the Merciful," said Rasulullah ﷺ. It was known that people were asked to changed their names if their names had any connotation of idolatry or paganism.

"As you command! I would sacrifice my mother and my father for you, O Messenger of Allah!" said the new 'Abd ar-Rahman ﷺ. This is a phrase that Arabs said when they really loved someone, because it would be unheard of to love anyone more than one's father and mother. People said this to the Prophet ﷺ very often, and they meant it. So the venerable *Sahabi's* ﷺ name was changed to 'Abd ar-Rahman, but this still was not the name by which people commonly called him.

There were many cats living in the *Masjid an-Nabawi* in those days, and of course there were many kittens as well. They used to hide in the long sleeves of Abd ar-Rahman's *jubba* (a long robe). In fact he was often seen with kittens all over him! Pretty soon everyone was calling him Abu Hurairah, the "father of a kitten." This name spread so far that it overtook both his other names.

In time, Abu Hurairah ﷺ became very close to the Messenger ﷺ, and the Prophet ﷺ gave him his own personal nickname. Instead of calling him Abu Hurairah, the Prophet ﷺ would call him Abu Hirr (*Hirr* means a fully grown cat). Having been given this nickname, Abu Hurairah ﷺ felt very close to Rasulullah ﷺ and he came to prefer "Abu Hirr" over "Abu Hurairah" because, he would say, "My beloved Rasulullah ﷺ used to call me by that name."

Abu Hurairah ﷺ had no wife or child in the lifetime of the Prophet ﷺ. Living in the *Masjid an-Nabawi*, he listened to everything that was said, took part in every act of worship, had the Prophet ﷺ as teacher and *Imam*, and devoted himself to worship, study, and the service of Rasulullah ﷺ.

The only relative that Abu Hurairah ﷺ had was his mother, who was very old. She insisted on following the old Arab faith, but Abu Hurairah ﷺ

never stopped talking to her about Islam. He was a dutiful son and he continued to love and serve her. But she kept rejecting his call to Islam and Abu Hurairah's 🕮 heart was filled with grief.

One day, as he was asking her to believe in Allah 🕮 and His Messenger 🕮, she called the Prophet 🕮 some bad names that hurt Abu Hurairah 🕮 deeply.

He went weeping to the Prophet 🕮, who asked, "What makes you cry, my Abu Hirr?"

"I am always calling my mother to Islam and she keeps refusing," he replied. "Today, I spoke to her again and she said things to me about you that deeply offended me. O Beloved Messenger, please ask Allah to soften her heart!"

The Prophet 🕮 was so moved that he made a *Du'a* for her right there.

What happened next was truly a miracle. As Abu Hurairah 🕮 told it, "I went home and found the door half-opened and heard water being poured. When I was about to go in, my mother said, "Stay where you are, Abu Hurairah."

She got dressed and told me to come in. I entered and she said, "I testify that there is no deity but Allah and that Muhammad is His worshipper and messenger..."

Abu Hurairah 🕮 returned to the Prophet 🕮,

with tears flowing from happiness, just as he had come an hour before crying from sadness. He said, "I bring you good news, O Rasulullah. Allah has responded to your *Du'a* and guided my mother to Islam..."

Sincere Love for the Prophet

Abu Hurairah's ﷺ love for the Prophet ﷺ was part of his very being. He could never get tired of looking upon the *nur* (light) of the Prophet's ﷺ face. He used to say, "I never saw anyone more handsome or more radiant than the Prophet ﷺ. It was as if the sun was in his face..."

He used to thank Allah ﷻ for allowing him to be a *Sahabi* of the Messenger ﷺ. He used to say, "Praise be to Allah Who guided me to Islam...Praise be to Allah Who taught me the Qur'an... Praise be to Allah Who granted me the companionship of Muhammad ﷺ..."

The Gift of a Special Memory

The *Sahabi* Zaid ibn Thabit ﷺ once said, "While Abu Hurairah and I were in the *Masjid* praying and remembering Allah, the Prophet ﷺ came to us and sat down. Out of respect we kept silent. But he said, 'Go back to what you were doing.'

"Before Abu Hurairah began, I started making a *Du'a* to which the Prophet ﷺ kept saying *'Amin.'*

"Then Abu Hurairah made a *Du'a,* saying: 'O Allah, I ask of You what my friend has asked of You, and I ask you for knowledge that is never to be forgotten.'

"The Prophet ﷺ again said, *'Amin.'*

"So I too prayed, 'I also ask you, O Allah, for knowledge never to be forgotten.'

"'The *Dawsi* man has come before you Zaid!' said the Prophet ﷺ in a jesting manner."

Because of the Prophet's ﷺ "*Amin,*" Abu Hurairah ؓ was able to remember everything he saw and heard for the rest of his life! If someone asked him what was recited in *Salah* the day before, he remembered. If someone asked exactly what Rasulullah ﷺ said about anything, he remembered. During the lifetime of the Prophet ﷺ, he became the reminder of the Muslims. Afterwards, when every word that could be recalled accurately was worth more than gold and diamonds, Abu Hurairah ؓ held a treasure which he passed on in the form of thousands of *Ahadith.*

The Prophet's Inheritance

Abu Hurairah ﷺ loved knowledge for himself and he loved it for others. Once he was passing through the markets of Madinah. He was saddened to see people so caught up in worldly affairs, completely absorbed with selling and buying. He stood before them and said, "How foolish you are, you people of Madinah!"

"What makes you say that, Abu Hurairah?" they asked.

"They are handing out the inheritance of the Prophet ﷺ and you are here?!" said Abu Hurairah ﷺ. "Why don't you go and take your share?"

"Who and where, O Abu Hurairah?" the people asked.

"In the *Masjid an-Nabawi*," replied the venerable *Sahabi* ﷺ.

All the people in the market rushed to the *Masjid* and Abu Hurairah ﷺ stood in the market waiting for them to come back.

When the people came back, they complained to him that they went to the *Masjid* and found nothing being handed out.

"Didn't you see anybody in the *Masjid*?" asked Abu Hurairah ﷺ.

"Yes," they said, "we saw people praying and reciting Qur'an. We saw people reminding each other to do good and avoid sins."

Abu Hurairah ☙ glanced at them all and said, "Don't you understand?! Don't you see?! That is the inheritance of our Blessed Messenger ﷺ!"

Sacrifice and Humility

Abu Hurairah ☙ lived in poverty. He endured hunger and suffering because of his devotion to knowledge and his desire to always be in the presence of Rasulullah ﷺ. He chose not to take work and to accept whatever food or clothing Allah ﷻ provided for him through the kindness of other Muslims. He thought that a normal life would stop him from spending all his time listening to and remembering the sayings and doings of Rasulullah ﷺ.

People tried to take care of him as well as the other homeless men of *Ahl-as-Suffah*. In the early days, many people were poor in Madinah and often there was very little to eat. The town had nearly doubled in size and those from Makkah had left everything they owned at home. So food, jobs and everything else had to stretch a long way. Many Arabs in those days had fewer luxuries than their neighbors and far fewer than people today.

Because of the scarcity of food, Abu Hurairah ☙ was often very hungry. He later said,

"Once I was so hungry that I tied a stone on my stomach to ease its pain. I sat at the entrance of the *Masjid*. Abu Bakr 🌸 passed by, and I asked him about some verse of the Qur'an, thinking he would take me home to eat, but he didn't.

"Then 'Umar 🌸 passed by and I asked about some verses, but he didn't invite me either. Then the Prophet 🌸 passed by. He knew how hungry I was. He said to me, 'Abu Hirr? Come.'

"'Yes, Rasulullah,' I replied, and I followed him. I entered the house with him. He found a cup of milk and asked his wife where it came from.

"'So-and-so sent it to you Rasulullah.'

"He turned to me and said, 'Go and call the men of *as-Suffah*!' I was very curious and wondered what this milk had do with *Ahl al-Suffah*. I was hoping to get some of it before I went, to give me some strength. But I went and invited *Ahl al-Suffah* and they came to the Prophet 🌸.

"He said, 'Take this, Abu Hurairah, and pass it around to them.' I kept giving each one the cup to drink, until every person was full. When they had all taken a drink, I gave the cup back to the Prophet 🌸. He raised his head and looked at me, smiling, and said, 'You and I are left.'

"'Yes, Rasulullah,' I replied, but I thought, 'How can this be? There surely can be no milk left.'

9

"'Drink,' he said, and I drank. Then he said, 'Drink,' and I drank. He kept saying so and I kept following until I said, 'I swear by the One Who sent you with the Truth that I am so full I cannot swallow any more.' So he took the cup and drank the rest."

Such was the miraculous nature of the Prophet Muhammad ﷺ.

Soon after that miracle, the treasures from the military expeditions began to pour into Madinah. Abu Hurairah ؓ received a stipend and a house. With these he was able to get married and raise a family.

Yet it didn't change a thing in his ؓ noble soul. He never forgot his past and would always recall it, saying, "I grew up without a father. I came to Madinah helpless. I worked for Busrah bint Ghazwan just to eat. I used to serve people when they came and bring their horses when they left..."

Many years later, the Muslim ruler Mu'awiyah ibn Abu Sufyan assigned Abu Hurairah ؓ to look after Madinah. Once, while he was governor, Abu Hurairah ؓ was passing through a narrow alley, carrying a load of firewood on his back. On his way he passed by Tha'labah ibn Malik ؓ, and said to him, "O Tha'labah, make way for the governor!"

Tha'labah ؓ replied, "May Allah bless you,

isn't all that space enough for you?"

"Make way for the governor," said Abu Hurairah ﷺ with a smile, "and for the heavy bundle of sticks he has on his back!" Though Abu Hurairah ﷺ was governor of the whole city of Madinah, he was still full of humility, and did not consider it beneath him to carry such a load upon his back.

Devotion to His Lord

In addition to his knowledge and concern for his community, Abu Hurairah ﷺ was a pious and humble person who remembered Allah ﷻ in all his daily actions and thoughts. He used to fast every other day and make *Nafl Salah* (supererogatory prayers) at every chance. He would pray the first third of the night and then wake up his wife to pray the second third. She would then wake up their daughter to pray the last third of the night.

In those later years, Abu Hurairah ﷺ had a maid-servant who insulted him by something she did. He raised his hand to hit her, but he stopped himself and said, "Had it not been for fear of the Day of Judgment, I would have retaliated in a way you did to me. But I'll sell you to the One ﷻ who pays me your price of which I am badly in need. Go, you are free, for the sake of Allah, the Almighty, so that He may free me from the Fire!"

True Generosity

Abu Hurairah's ﷺ daughter used to say to him, "O Father, girls tease me. They say, 'Why doesn't your father let you wear gold?'"

"O Daughter," he said, "Tell them: 'My father fears for me the heat of the fire.'"

Abu Hurairah ﷺ didn't refuse his daughter gold out of stinginess. He did this because he wanted to prevent her from becoming attached to worldly things. He himself was very generous in the way of Allah ﷻ. Once, one of the Umayyad *Khulafa'* sent a servant to him with one hundred golden *dinars*. The next day, the *Khalifah* sent his servant again with the message: "My servant gave you the *dinars* by mistake; you were not the one meant to have them."

Abu Hurairah ﷺ answered him, "I spent it all in the way of Allah; I haven't a single one of your *dinars* left in my house. When my share of the Muslim treasury is due, take your money from it." The *Khalifah* only did this to test the honesty of Abu Hurairah ﷺ. He investigated the matter and it was true. All the gold had been given away in one day.

The Dutiful Son

All his life, Abu Hurairah ﷺ remained devoted to his mother. Each time he wanted to go out, he stood at her door and said, "*As-salamu 'alaiki*, O Mother, *wa rahmatullahi wa barakatuhu.*"

And she would answer, "*Wa 'alaika as-salam*, O Son, *wa rahmatullahi wa barakatuhu.*"

He would say, "May Allah bless you, for you protected me when I was young."

And she would say, "May Allah bless you, for you took care of me when you grew up."

Then, when he came back home, he would say the same.

Abu Hurairah ﷺ always insisted on calling people to love their parents and keep warm, close connections with all their relatives. Once, he saw two men walking, one older than the other. The younger did not appear to be showing proper respect for the elder. Abu Hurairah ﷺ said to the younger one, "What is the relation of this man to you?"

"He is my father," replied the younger man.

Abu Hurairah ﷺ then advised him: "Show respect. Don't call him by his first name... Don't walk in front of him... Don't sit in front of him..."

Looking to the Next World

When Abu Hurairah ﷺ was dying, he wept. The people present asked him what caused him to cry. He answered them, "I am not crying for your world...I am crying because the trip is too long and the provision is too little...I am now standing at the end of a way which looks onto Heaven or Hell...I don't know in which I will be!"

The Umayyad ruler Marwan visited him at that time and said, "May Allah cure you, Abu Hurairah!"

"O Allah," said Abu Hurairah ﷺ, "I love to meet You so may You love meeting me as well and do it soon..."

Marwan had hardly left when Abu Hurairah ﷺ passed into the next life.

May Allah ﷻ bless Abu Hurairah ﷺ. He preserved for the Muslims over five thousand three hundred Ahadith of the Prophet ﷺ. May Allah ﷻ reward him with the best for what he did for Islam and the Muslims.

Abu Sufyan
ibn al-Harith

"Look at him: he is the first to come to the masjid and the last to leave, always looking at his feet."
Rasulullah ﷺ

bu Sufyan was born at nearly the same time as the Prophet ﷺ and they were raised in the same family. He was his closest cousin, for the father of Abu Sufyan and the father of the Prophet ﷺ were both sons of 'Abdul-Muttalib. He was not only a cousin but also a close friend to the young Muhammad ﷺ and they very much resembled each other. The Prophet of Allah ﷺ and Abu Sufyan ibn al-Harith were foster-brothers. When they were nursing as babies, Halimah as-Sa'diyyah ﷺ used to provide both of them with her milk.

And yet Allah ﷻ calls whom He wills to the Truth. While one friend was receiving the direct message of Allah ﷻ in his heart, the other received nothing, and turned against his cousin entirely. When the Messenger ﷺ called his close family to Islam, ibn Harith's soul turned against him. Friendship turned to dislike, kinship to separation and brotherhood to alienation.

Abu Sufyan ibn al-Harith ﷜ had become, by that time, one of the most famous warriors among the Quraish. He decided to put all of his energy into opposing the Muslims. He had also become a noted poet, and likewise dedicated his clever tongue to mocking the Prophet ﷺ and opposing his call. His terrible prose was meant to offend and insult the Prophet ﷺ. Ibn Harith called him all kinds of foul and obscene names. This greatly hurt the Prophet's ﷺ feelings because ibn Harith used to be such a close and good friend.

Abu Sufyan ibn al-Harith's anger with Rasulullah ﷺ lasted nearly twenty years. During this time he took every opportunity to conspire against him and to hurt the Muslims. He helped to drive them out of Makkah and he would have been happy to see them all die in Madinah.

From Darkness to Light

The Muslim community became very strong in Madinah. Nourished by the chance to establish a real Islamic community, and constantly inspired by the presence of Rasulullah ﷺ, they were miraculously powerful in battle and radiantly beautiful in peace. More and more people came to see that what the Muslims had was much better than their own lives. The tribes began to pledge allegiance to the Prophet ﷺ. Slowly the Muslims gained strength, until their biggest enemies, the Quraish of Makkah, were genuinely afraid; and well they might be. The Quraish had fought the Muslims for a long time, and they feared they would receive no mercy if the Muslims decided to come to Makkah and attack.

At last the Prophet ﷺ gathered the Muslims into an army. He did not tell anyone but his closest companions where he was taking them, but even so, the largest army ever seen in Arabia gathered simply for the honor of accompanying him wherever he went. The great army marched into the desert, and one thought they were going to this place, another to that. Only after marching for some days did they turn towards Makkah, and their purpose became clear.

Meanwhile, in Makkah, there was news of

the approaching great force and rumors and suspicions began to arise. Those people who had been wavering between Islam and disbelief decided for Islam. Who can blame them; Allah ﷻ uses fear as well as love to open the human heart. Some of them became famous Muslims after that. Among these were 'Abbas ﷺ, the uncle of Rasulullah ﷺ (some say he was secretly Muslim all along, and Allah ﷻ knows best), and Abu Sufyan ibn Harb, the leading chief of the city. And yet another was the subject of this story, the Prophet's ﷺ own cousin, Abu Sufyan ibn al-Harith ﷺ.

Ibn Harith ﷺ told the story of his entering Islam with these moving words:

> When Islam became fully established and we heard the news that Rasulullah ﷺ was heading for Makkah to take it, I felt such despair. I said: "Where shall I go? Whom shall I accompany? With whom shall I be?!"
>
> I went to my wife and my children and said: "Prepare yourself to leave Makkah because Muhammad is about to appear. If the Muslims get hold of me, I am a dead man."
>
> "Can't you see," my family replied, "that the Arabs and even foreigners now follow Muhammad and embrace his religion? Why do you insist on your hatred for him while you

should have been the first to support him and protect him?"

They kept trying to soften my heart and tempt me to adopt the religion of Muhammad ﷺ until Allah opened my heart to Islam.

I jumped up at once and told my servant to prepare a camel and a horse for us. I took my son Ja'far with me and rushed to al-Abu'a, a place between Makkah and Madinah, where I was told the Prophet ﷺ was camped.

When I came near the camp, I disguised myself for fear of being recognized and killed before I reached the Prophet ﷺ and declared my Islam.

I continued walking for about a mile and the Muslim warriors were going in the direction of Makkah, one group after the other. I kept hiding from them for fear of being recognized.

While I was walking, the Prophet ﷺ appeared. I crossed to him, stood before him and took the veil off my face. When he saw me and recognized me, he turned his face to the other direction, so I went to the other direction and again he turned his face. I kept standing before him and he kept turning away from me.

I had thought that he ﷺ would be happy with my entering Islam and that his companions would be happy because of his happiness.

But when the Muslims saw him ignoring me, they frowned and avoided me too. Abu Bakr ﷺ turned away abruptly, so I looked to 'Umar ibn al-Khattab ﷺ, trying to touch his heart, but he was even more determined to scorn me. He even provoked one of the *Ansar* against me. That man then said: "O enemy of Allah, you hurt Rasulullah ﷺ and his companions! Everyone from east to west knows of your hatred for the Prophet ﷺ!" The *Ansar* man kept insulting me and shouting at me and the Muslim warriors were looking at me, pleased with what was happening.

At that point, I saw my uncle 'Abbas. I sought help from him and said, "O Uncle, I hoped that Muhammad would be happy with my entering Islam for my kinship and my noble birth. But you just saw what he did. Please speak to him so that he might accept me."

But 'Abbas replied, "By Allah, I will never say a word to him after I saw his avoidance of you. Only if an opportunity appears will I do so, for I follow the Prophet ﷺ and love him."

"O Uncle," I said, "who will help me if you don't?" 'Abbas sternly replied, "I owe you nothing but what you just heard." So I felt overwhelmed by grief and hopelessness. Soon after, I met my cousin 'Ali ibn Abi Talib. I talked to him and he gave me the same response that I received from 'Abbas.

I went back to my uncle 'Abbas in desperation and cried, "O Uncle, if you can't make Muhammad ﷺ forgive me, at least stop the man who is insulting me and encouraging others to do so."

"What man? Describe him to me," he said and I did. "Ah...That would be Nu'aiman an-Najjari. Yes, I will do that for you," he said. 'Abbas went to Nu'aiman saying, "O Nu'aiman, ibn Harith is the first cousin of Rasulullah ﷺ and my nephew. If the Prophet ﷺ is angry with him now, some day he will be satisfied with him, so leave him alone." 'Abbas kept telling him that until he stopped the insults and said, "Very well, I won't bother him any more."

When the Prophet ﷺ and the army camped in al-Jahfah (another place between Madinah and Makkah), I sat at the entrance of his tent with my young son Ja'far. As the Prophet ﷺ was coming out he saw me and shunned me. I did not give up though. Everywhere he went, I sat at the entrance of his tent with my son Ja'far, and each time he saw me, he turned his face away.

I remained this way for a long time. When I could not stand it any more I said, "By

Allah, Rasulullah must let me in his tent or I will take this little boy of mine and go wandering the desert until we die from hunger and thirst!" When the Prophet ﷺ heard these words he felt sorry for us. He let us into the tent, forgave me and accepted our entrance into Islam.

When Rasulullah ﷺ and the Muslim army entered Makkah, I was with him. He went to the *Ka'ba* and I went to make *Sa'i* with him. I did not leave him for a single moment.

On the day of the Battle of Hunain, the Arab tribes that lived to the east of Makkah had gathered to fight the Prophet ﷺ as they had never gathered before, and they mobilized an army like no one ever had, since they wished to destroy, finally, Islam and the Muslims.

The Prophet ﷺ went to meet them with the Muslim army, and I went along with them. When I saw the large number of *kuffar,* I said to myself: "By Allah, I shall atone for all my previous hatred to the Prophet ﷺ and he will be happy with me."

The Muslims attacked but the enemy was very hard on them. The Muslim line started to collapse. We retreated around the Prophet ﷺ and were about to suffer a terrible defeat.

But the Prophet ﷺ - may I sacrifice my mother and my father for him - remained firmly in the heart of the battle. He was sitting on his mule like a great solid mountain, fighting with his sword. When I saw that, I broke the sheath of my sword so that I could not put it away. I prepared myself to die for him.

My uncle 'Abbas held the reins of the mule and stood next to Rasulullah ﷺ. I stood on the other side with my sword in my right hand and my left hand holding his stirrup.

When Rasulullah ﷺ saw me fighting so bravely, he asked 'Abbas: "Who is that?" He did not recognize me since I was wearing a chain mail cover over my face. "That is your first cousin, Abu Sufyan ibn al-Harith," answered my uncle, "so please be finally pleased with him, O Rasulullah." "I am," said the Blessed Prophet ﷺ, "and now Allah too has forgiven him all his previous wrong actions."

I was so happy to hear these words. He ﷺ turned to me and said, "O my cousin, fight! Fight!" These words of Rasulullah ﷺ greatly encouraged me. I lunged so hard on the enemy soldiers that they began to pull back and all the Muslims attacked with me until we drove the enemy away and sent them running in every direction.

True Devotion

From the day of the Battle of Hunain, Abu Sufyan ibn al-Harith ﷺ was in good standing with the Prophet ﷺ and enjoyed his noble company, but he never did look him in the eye, because he was ashamed of his past.

He wrote these verses about his life in the *Jahiliyyah* times:

> *I was like one going astray in the darkness*
> *of the night,*
> *But now I am led on the Right Path.*
> *I could not guide myself, and he who, with*
> *Allah, overcame me,*
> *Was he whom I had driven away with all*
> *my might.*

Abu Sufyan ibn al-Harith ﷺ deeply regretted those years of darkness that he spent in the *Jahiliyyah*, deprived of the Light of Allah ﷻ and His Messenger ﷺ. So after he became a Muslim he devoted himself, night and day, to reciting the Qur'an and understanding Islam. He turned his back to this world and its pleasures and sought Allah ﷻ devotedly and with much humility.

Once Rasulullah ﷺ saw him entering the *Masjid* and said to 'A'ishah ﷺ: "Do you know who that is, 'A'ishah?"

"No, Rasulullah," she replied.

"It's my cousin, ibn al-Harith. Look at him: he is the first to come to the *Masjid* and the last to leave, always looking at his shoes [out of humility]."

When Rasulullah ﷺ passed away, Abu Sufyan ibn al-Harith ﷺ mourned for him deeply. He lamented his death in a mournful poem full of grief and anguish.

During the *Khilafah* of 'Umar ibn al-Khattab ﷺ, Abu Sufyan ibn al-Harith ﷺ dug his own grave with his own hands. Three days later, he lay on his deathbed; it was as if he had known he was soon to have his appointment with death. He said to his wife and children:

"Don't cry for me. By Allah, I have not committed a major sin since I became Muslim..." He then passed away. 'Umar ﷺ prayed over his body and he and all the rest of the noble *Sahabah* felt grief after losing him.

The story of Abu Sufyan ibn al-Harith's ﷺ life reminds us that change is within us, and that at any point in our life we can turn from good to bad or from bad to good. He turned from opposition to acceptance. His heart melted from stubbornness to surrender.

May Allah ﷺ be pleased with him.

'Adi ibn Hatim at-Ta'i

"You believed as they disbelieved, you accepted as they denied, you have been loyal as they betrayed, you came as they turned away."
'Umar ibn al-Khattab

For the people of old Arabia, nothing was more beloved than a good story, poem or song. Certain famous people, who were known for having a special quality such as great bravery, or beauty, or generosity, had songs and stories and poems written about them. These were passed on from person to person and became part of the language and culture of the Arabs.

One of those about whom people loved to write and hear was Hatim at-Ta'i. He was the best known of all the desert people for his extraordinary generosity. Tales of his kindness to strangers and his willingness to give up all he had were even recited during his lifetime. After he died, these stories continued to be told, and people even invented new tales about him. Many of these stories about the generosity of Hatim at-Ta'i are still very much a part of Arab folklore and literature today.

When Hatim at-Ta'i died, he left a son named 'Adi to inherit the position as chief of the tribe. But 'Adi was not as generous as his famous father had been. He took a quarter of the wealth of the people for himself, since this was the accepted custom of Arab chieftains of his day.

When Rasulullah ﷺ declared his mission, he began calling the Arabs to guidance and truth. Over time, the many Arab tribes slowly joined him, one after the other. When Islam became established in the city of Madinah, the people of the desert (the bedouins) saw the growing power of the Muslims. They made alliances with the Prophet ﷺ and began to come into Islam at a greater rate. But not so the tribe of Ta'i.

'Adi saw in the remarkable leadership of Rasulullah ﷺ the end of his own power. He was not willing to surrender his power to anyone else. He was not willing to surrender himself to Allah ﷻ. So he came to despise Rasulullah ﷺ, even though he had never met him. This hostility lasted for nearly twenty years, until his heart was opened to the message of Allah ﷻ in the ninth year of the *Hijrah*.

How 'Adi came to this remarkable change of heart is best told in his own words:

No Arab hated the Prophet ﷺ more than I did. I was a chief of noble birth and I used to travel about among my people to collect a quarter of their stock. I was a Christian and I was my own master in religious matters; I was a king among my people and I was treated like a king. I wanted no part of this "new prophet" and his new religion.

When the Muslims became stronger, and their warriors were everywhere, east and west in the Arab lands, I told one of my servants, "Get some of the best of my camels ready and tie them somewhere nearby. If you hear that a group of Muhammad's followers has come to this area, let me know immediately."

One day, the servant came to me saying that whatever I intended to do when Muhammad's troops arrived, I had better do it now. He had seen battle flags way in the distance. He asked about them and was told it was the army of Muhammad ﷺ.

So I told him to get our camels ready and bring them to me. I took my whole family and left that land, which we all loved, and ran away, heading for Syria where we could live with other Christians.

I was in such a great hurry. When we had passed beyond the threatened area, I discovered that I had left a sister of mine with those who remained in Ta'i. There was no way to go back, so I went forward to Syria and lived there with people of my religion.

What happened to my sister was exactly what I had expected and feared, except that the end of the story was not expected at all. I heard all about it from travelers and witnesses who were there.

First, news reached me in Syria that the army of Muhammad ﷺ had taken my sister, along with other captives, to Madinah. There, they were all put in a place near the *Masjid an-Nabawi*. I supposed they were being kept for ransom. From these captives, the Prophet ﷺ heard about my flight to Syria.

When Rasulullah ﷺ passed by the captives, my sister stood up politely and said, "O Rasulullah, my father has died, and the person responsible for me after him is no longer in at-Ta'i, so I have no one to protect me and pay a ransom for my release. Please grant me mercy so that Allah will grant it to you."

"Who is that missing person of yours?" asked the Prophet ﷺ.

"'Adi ibn Hatim," she replied.

"Ah, the one who ran away from Allah and His Prophet!" said Rasulullah ﷺ. Then he left her and went on his way.

The next day he passed by again. She repeated what she had said the day before and he repeated what he had said also.

The day after that he passed by again, but she didn't say anything because she had lost hope. But someone behind the Prophet ﷺ made her a sign to go and talk to him, so she did.

She said, "O Rasulullah, my father has died, and the person responsible for me after him is no longer there, so I have no one to protect me and pay ransom for my release. Please grant me mercy so that Allah will grant it to you."

The Prophet ﷺ said, "Come! I give you your freedom."

She said, "I want to go to my family in Syria."

Rasulullah ﷺ replied, "But you must not leave before you find some trustworthy man from your tribe who can take you to Syria. Whenever you find him, let me know."

When the Prophet ﷺ left, she asked who

the man was who had signaled her to talk to Rasulullah ﷺ one more time. She was told that he was 'Ali ibn Abi Talib ﷺ.

She stayed there in Madinah until she recognized some travelers passing on their way north. Then she went to the Prophet ﷺ and said, "O Rasulullah, some of my people have come. They are trustworthy and they can take me with them."

So the Prophet ﷺ gave her clothes, a camel and enough money for the trip and she left with her people.

We kept seeking news of her, waiting for her arrival. We couldn't believe that Muhammad ﷺ had treated her so gently, knowing my hostility towards him. He could have kept her for a high ransom, or made her a slave. By Allah, I was sitting with my family when I saw a woman coming towards us riding in a covered seat on her camel. I said, "This is the daughter of Hatim," and so she was.

As soon as she saw me, she said, "You cut the bonds of kinship and you are unfair. You took your own family and your children and abandoned your father's children!"

I said, "O little sister, don't say such hurtful things! You're right and I have no excuse!" I kept trying to apologize to her, and make up with her, until at last things were reconciled between us. She got down from her camel and stayed with us.

She told her story. I knew she was a wise woman, so I asked her about Muhammad ﷺ. I wanted to know her opinion of him. She said, "I think that you must join him quickly. If he is a prophet, the people near him will be preferred. If he is just a king, you will never be humiliated there, being who you are."

I prepared myself and left south for Madinah. I reached the Prophet ﷺ with no guarantee of protection. I knew that he had said, "I hope Allah will put the hand of 'Adi in my hand."

I entered the *Masjid* and gave him my greetings. He said, "Who is this man?"

I said, "'Adi ibn Hatim at-Ta'i."

He stood up, held my hand, and took me home with him. On our way, an old frail woman with a little boy stopped him with a complaint. He spoke with her for some time, until her problem was solved.

I then thought to myself, "By God, this is no king."

Then we went to his home. There he took a leather pillow stuffed with dry grass, gave it to me, and said, "Sit on this!"

I was ashamed and said, "No, you sit on it." He said, "No, you."

I obeyed and sat on it while Rasulullah ﷺ sat on the ground since there was no other pillow in his home.

I told myself, "By God, this is not the way a king behaves!"

The Prophet ﷺ turned to me and said, "You are not a very good Christian are you?" I said very humbly, "Why do you say that?"

"Weren't you taking a quarter of the belongings of the people for yourself, although that is forbidden in your religion?"

I said, "Yes," and then I knew that he was a prophet sent by Allah, for how else could he know that I did such a thing?

Then he ﷺ said, "Maybe, 'Adi, what you see of the poverty of the Muslims is keeping you from entering Islam. By Allah, soon so much money will flow in that there won't be any to take it.

"Or maybe, 'Adi, what is keeping you is the small number of Muslims and the great number of their enemies. By Allah, soon you will hear that a woman can come from a village in Iraq to visit the *Ka'bah* on her own and no one will bother her.

"Or maybe you see power and authority

with the great emperors. By Allah, soon you will hear that Muslims have conquered Iraq with its castles and that the treasures of Khosraw son of Hormuz belong to them."

I said, "The treasures of Khosraw son of Hormuz?" He said, "Yes, the treasures of Khosraw son of Hormuz."

Thereupon I made the *Shahadah* and became Muslim.

'Adi ibn Hatim at-Ta'i ﷺ lived a long time after that and he used to say, "Two of the Prophet's ﷺ predictions have come true, and the third yet remains. By Allah, I swear it too will come true.

"I have seen women coming from Iraq to Makkah on camels, on their own, unafraid to make the *Hajj*, fearing nothing but Allah.

"And I was among the first troops that attacked Khosraw and opened the treasures of his castles. I swear by Allah, the third is coming!"

The third prediction of the Blessed Prophet ﷺ came to pass at the time of the pious *Khalifah* 'Umar ibn 'Abd al-'Aziz ﷺ. The Muslims' wealth was so abundant that they used to call for poor to take *Zakah* and nobody came to take it.

May Allah ﷻ bless 'Adi ibn Hatim at-Ta'i ﷺ and reward him for his ability to see the Truth.

'Ammar ibn 'Abasah

"When you hear that I have conquered you may come to me, wherever I may be."
Rasulullah ﷺ

There was once a time when there were very few Muslims on the face of the earth. There were, however, men and women here and there who believed in One God and remembered something of the original teachings of the Prophet Ibrahim ﷺ. A person who believed in the Oneness of Allah ﷻ as Ibrahim ﷺ had taught was called a *Hanif* (the plural of which is *Hunafa'*). These *Hunafa'* were always searching for the best way to worship Allah ﷻ, for though they knew He was there, they did not know how He wanted to be worshipped.

This was the spiritual station of Rasulullah ﷺ before the Revelation on Mount Hira. He went many times up into the caves to meditate. He would fast and ponder on the life of this world and the next. The Angel Jibril ﷺ finally came to him and taught him the true way of reaching Allah ﷻ.

After Rasulullah ﷺ began teaching others about Islam, from time to time one of the *Hunafa'* would hear of the Prophet ﷺ and immediately recognize the truth of his message. This is the story of such a one.

The Early Days of Islam

It was the fourth year after Rasulullah ﷺ had started receiving the Revelation. Up until this time, Islam was being spread quietly, among the family and intimate friends of Rasulullah ﷺ. But now, the quiet time of the first three years was over. The period of open preaching, of *Da'wah*, had arrived. With it however came the violent, hateful, oppressive and cruel torment of the pagans among the Quraish. Ironically, these were the same people who, before the Revelation, had considered Muhammad ibn 'Abdullah ﷺ to be the best among them, the most honest, upright and truthful. They now all turned completely against him for their own selfish reasons.

But the early Muslims were steadfast. They withstood torture and death because they knew without a doubt that Allah ﷻ would reward them and that what they believed in was surely the Truth.

Rasulullah ﷺ kept going out, day after day, to teach the people of Makkah as Allah ﷻ had ordered him to do. He would go wherever he could find groups of people, not only Makkans but groups of visitors, traders, and shoppers.

There were several occasions every year in Arabia which drew people from hundreds of miles around. One was the Pilgrimage to the *Ka'bah* in Makkah. During this time, there were several great poetry contests as well as the great trading fair of 'Ukaz.

A Blessed Exchange at the Market

One day Rasulullah ﷺ went to the fair of 'Ukaz, accompanied by Abu Bakr as-Siddiq and Bilal ﷺ. There they found people from every corner of Arabia buying, selling, eating, drinking, singing, arguing, bargaining, and doing all sorts of business. The Prophet ﷺ found a good place to stand and started to invite the people to hasten to Islam. As usual, the unbelievers gathered around him in a mob and started to insult him. They shouted in order to drown out his sweet voice. They made fun of him and his followers and they even threw stones and garbage at him.

In the midst of this crowd was a bedouin, a nomad from the desert, who had come to the fair to trade some of his animals, leather goods and wool for things his family needed. This bedouin was very impressed with the dignified way the speaker stood up to the mob. He watched and listened for a while, and when the crowd became tired of its rude sport and went away to bother someone else, he approached Rasulullah ﷺ and began to ask him questions.

"Who are you?" asked the bedouin.

"I am the Messenger of Allah," he ﷺ replied.

"What is a Messenger of Allah?" the bedouin asked.

"One who brings the Lord God's words to the people," replied Rasulullah ﷺ.

"Has Allah really sent you down?"

"Yes, Allah has made me His Prophet."

"What is your message?"

"Believe in one God. Do not associate anyone with Him; do not worship idols. Love your relatives and treat them well."

"Has anybody believed you?" asked the bedouin, who by now was really interested.

"One free man and a slave have believed me," said the Prophet 鐌, pointing to his two companions, Abu Bakr and Bilal 鐌.

"What is this 'Islam' I heard you mention?" inquired the bedouin.

"Islam means to behave with everyone with good manners and to feed the poor and the needy. Islam means submission to Allah and being steadfast in His cause."

"What is the noblest act of Islam?"

"That nobody should hurt anybody verbally or physically."

"O Prophet of Allah!" cried the bedouin, "I also believe in this. I believe in one God. I reject idol worship. Good behavior with relatives could be the motto of my life."

Rasulullah 鐌 looked at the bedouin and asked his name. He said his name was Abu Najib 'Ammar ibn 'Abasah.

"Abu Najib," said Rasulullah 鐌, "the cruelties we must bear lie beyond your endurance. For the time being, you may go back to your home. When you hear that I have gained the upper hand, you may come to me, wherever I may be."

Abu Najib 鐌 returned to his native region with a treasure, the blessings of this world and the next. He remembered all of what Rasulullah 鐌 had said that day and vowed to put it into practice.

An Early Inclination to Truth

Later it was learned that Abu Najib ﷺ had left the worship of idols by the time he had become a man, long before he had even met Rasulullah ﷺ. Even as a young boy, he had understood from his heart that idols neither help nor harm anyone. He had known that the idol-worshippers around him were confused and mistaken.

After some time, Abu Najib ﷺ met someone of the People of the Book, a Jew or a Christian, who had explained to him that their records contained a prophecy about the coming of a new prophet. He would come from Makkah, the man said. He would keep the people away from the worship of idols and invite them to worship the One unseen God. The prophecies said that his law would be better than the other laws before it.

After talking to this man from the People of the Book, Abu Najib ﷺ had always been on the lookout for people from Makkah. Every time he found someone from that city, he would inquire about the news of the place. One day, a traveler from Makkah had informed him that there was a man who was trying to keep the people from idol-worship and he was teaching them about the worship of one great God. The reporter had thought highly of the decency of this man, and how his manner of speaking alone clearly showed he was pointing the way to a higher and better way of life.

Abu Najib ﷺ said that as soon as he heard this, he climbed onto his camel. "In the `Ukaz market, I found the Prophet ﷺ and presented myself to him. I then put some questions to him. Being satisfied with the answers, I accepted Islam. The Prophet ﷺ knew that my tribe robbed and even killed travelers. He instructed me to go back to my native place and prevent robbing and killing on the public roads and maintain peace."

Abu Najib 'Ammar ibn 'Abasah ﷺ was one of the unusual people amongst the Arabs to discover, even before he met Rasulullah ﷺ, that Allah ﷺ is One.

May Allah ﷺ be pleased
with Abu Najib 'Ammar ibn Abasah ﷺ.

44

'Amr ibn al-Jamuh

"I witness that he is walking here and there in Paradise and his lame leg is set right."
Rasulullah ﷺ

During the *Jahiliyyah* days, or the Days of Ignorance, when Madinah was still called Yathrib, the inhabitants of this city used to worship many idols. Islam had not yet come to Yathrib and its people thought that these idols were partners with Allah ﷻ. They made statues of these "gods" and people liked to have these statues in their homes. After a time, they began to worship the statues themselves. They believed them to have magical powers and they believed that they could hear and sometimes even speak.

One of the people who believed in idols was a man named 'Amr ibn al-Jamuh. He was very serious about his belief. His idol, which was named Manat, was made of the most expensive wood of the day. It was kept in a special room which was only for the purpose of its worship. He took very good care of it, perfuming it with the most exquisite scents, rubbing it with oils and burning incense before it. He used to make sacrifices to it and seek its help at difficult moments in his life.

Now 'Amr was one of the leaders of Yathrib in the time of *Jahiliyyah*. He became the chief of Banu Salamah. He was also one of the most generous and valiant men of the city. He was a kind and responsible person. But he couldn't bear any criticism of his idol or of his love for it. He went on worshipping it most of his life. When he was already an old man, over sixty, with white hair and a lame foot, Islam started penetrating the homes of Yathrib. One after the other, its citizens embraced Islam through the first ambassador, Mus'ab ibn 'Umair ﷺ.

'Amr's three sons, Mu'awwadh, Mu'adh and Khallad became Muslims at Mus'ab's hand, as did a friend of theirs named Mu'adh ibn Jabal ﷺ. 'Amr's son Mu'adh ﷺ was even one of those who went to take the hand of Rasulullah ﷺ at the second covenant of al-'Aqabah. Not only had 'Amr's sons accepted Islam; even his wife Hind ﷺ had become a Muslim. But 'Amr did not know about all of this.

Hind ﷺ saw that Islam had won over the people of Yathrib, and that only her husband and a few others were left unconvinced. She loved and respected her husband very much and feared that he might die in a state of *Kufr* (unbelief) and end up in the Fire. She and her three sons were very worried about him.

At the same time, 'Amr was afraid that his children would abandon their ancestors' religion to follow the teachings of Mus'ab ibn 'Umair ﷺ. Mus'ab ﷺ was so convincing that he had, within a short span of time, persuaded a lot of people to turn away from their old religion to the faith of the Prophet ﷺ. He was determined to keep his family worshipping in the old way, which he thought was best.

He said to his wife, "Make sure, Hind, that none of your sons meets this man Mus'ab before we can make a final opinion of him ourselves."

This put Hind ﷺ in a difficult position. She could not lie to her husband, but she wanted him to understand what was happening. So she replied, "I will. But concerning this man, can't you just hear what your son Mu'adh has to say?"

'Amr was very upset, and said in a loud voice, "Has Mu'adh turned away from our religion without talking things over with me?!"

The woman felt sad for her husband, who was so sincere, and said, "Not at all. He has only attended some of his meetings and memorized some of his sayings."

'Amr told her to bring their son at once. When he came, 'Amr asked him to recite some of the sayings of the man from Makkah. His son, very happy that at least his father was ready to discuss the subject, recited *al-Fatihah*.

After he had heard it, 'Amr was truly impressed. "How perfect these words are and how beautiful! Is everything that he says as good as this?"

Mu'adh ؓ replied, "Yes, Father. It would be wonderful if you would follow him. All of your family already has!"

The old man was silent. After a while he said, "I must consult our goddess Manat and see what she says."

The son asked, "What can Manat say, Father? It is only a piece of wood. It can't think, it can't speak...it can't do anything."

Because he sensed disrespect in his son, the old man repeated with anger, "I said I shall consult her!"

Tricked toward the Truth

So 'Amr went to the idol of Manat. It was the tradition of the people of Yathrib that when they wanted the advice of the idol, they used to place a certain woman behind a curtain that was in back of the idol. She was supposed to go into a trance and then say what the idol would inspire her to say. 'Amr called for this woman and then prepared to stand before his idol. What he did not know was that his wife had met the woman outside and drove her away from the house.

'Amr stood before his idol on his lame foot. After praising it he said, "O Manat, you surely know that this man who came from Makkah is your enemy. He came to turn us away from you. I don't want to follow him without consulting you, although his sayings are beautiful. So advise me what to do."

But Manat did not answer. So 'Amr continued to talk and to ask questions. No reply came. At last he decided to let the idol wait for a few days. Perhaps it was angry. He thought he would put off any decision until later.

'Amr's sons knew how attached their father was to Manat. It was like a part of him. They didn't want to hurt their respected father, who was indeed a very good man. But they knew that his soul was at stake. They realized that the idol's power over him was shaken, and that they might be able to take it away by force and thus open his path to Islam.

By this time, Rasulullah ﷺ had come to Yathrib and they felt even stronger in their convictions. So they decided to act. Being young men, they thought of a very funny solution.

'Amr's sons and their friend Mu'adh ibn Jabal ﷺ came late at night to the special room where the idol was kept. They were very quiet so as not to wake anybody. They took the idol Manat and threw it into the sewage pit belonging to their tribe, Banu Salamah. They then hurried back home without being seen. They went to sleep, looking forward to what might happen.

The next morning, 'Amr went to give morning greetings to his idol, but he found it missing. He asked who had attacked his idol by night but nobody answered. He searched for it everywhere, indoors, outdoors, shouting and threatening, until at last he found it lying face down in the filthy sewage pit.

He cleaned the idol, purified and perfumed it lovingly, then put it back in its place and said, "Truly, if I only knew who did this to you, I would beat him very severely!"

The next night the young men crept into the

house and took Manat again, and again the next morning the old man searched for it and found it in the dirty hole and cleaned it. The young men kept doing so every night until 'Amr got really angry. He then hung a sword around the idol's neck and said, "O Manat, I don't know who is doing this to you but if you have any power, defend yourself! Here is a sword for you!" And he went to sleep.

When the sons and their friend were sure that the father was asleep, they took the sword off the idol's neck. Then they tied the idol with a rope to a dead dog. They threw them both into the dirty pit.

In the morning, the old man found his idol lying face down, tied to a dead dog in the pit. It was without the sword. This time he left it where it lay and cursed it, saying, "You cannot even defend yourself! How can you be a god?! You are nothing but a piece of wood." Later that day he accepted Islam.

'Amr ﷺ was an eloquent poet. After he realized the foolishness of idol-worship he composed these verses:

By God! Had you been a goddess then the dead dog would not have been tied to you with a rope in a pit.

Curses be on you - you were lying in a filthy

place. How wretched was that place!

Had I not been there to save you, you would have been there still, upside down.

Allah, the Glorified, guided me before I was sent to the darkness of the grave.

All praises for Allah Most Great Who is Benefactor, Provider and Lord of the Day of Judgment!

'Amr's ﷺ Desire to Meet His Lord

When 'Amr ﷺ tasted the sweetness of Islam, he regretted very much the time he had wasted in idolatry. He went, full of enthusiasm, and placed his body, his soul, his money and his sons at the service of Allah ﷻ and His Messenger ﷺ.

Before long, 'Amr ﷺ saw his sons preparing themselves to confront the enemies of Islam, looking forward to obtaining martyrdom in the Battle of Uhud. Seeing this, 'Amr's heart was on fire to join them, and he decided to go with them on *Jihad* under the leadership of Rasulullah ﷺ. But the young men were against this. Not only was he too old but he was also crippled with a lame foot.

They told him that surely Allah ﷻ would excuse him for his age and his lameness. Why would he take this burden on himself when Allah ﷻ had exempted him? Out of their fear for his life, they continued arguing with him. However, their father would not listen to them at all.

'Amr's sons went to Rasulullah ﷺ and told him the situation. The Prophet ﷺ said they could explain to their father that due to his age and condition, he was not obligated to perform *Jihad.*

The young men said that they had done their best to explain this to their father, but he wouldn't listen. Rasulullah ﷺ then asked them to bring their father to him, so that he might explain that he need not fight, and that hopefully Allah ﷻ would reward his intention.

'Amr ؓ, determined to stand by his decision, went to the Prophet ﷺ, complaining, "O Rasulullah, my sons want to keep me away from the source of Goodness, arguing that I am crippled. By Allah, I hope to step into *Jannah* with my lame foot! For the sake of Allah, allow me to accompany you!"

Rasulullah ﷺ said to the sons, "Let him go. Maybe Allah will grant him martyrdom."

And they obeyed. Joyfully, the venerable old man returned to his home and prepared for battle. When the time came to go out, 'Amr ؓ said a last goodbye to his wife. Then he turned towards the *Qiblah,* raised his hands and said, "O Allah, bless me with martyrdom; do not send me back to my family with my hopes dashed!" Then he took off with his three sons and a large number of his people, the Banu Salamah.

The battle raged at the foot of Mount 'Uhud and, after some time, it turned against the Muslims. Many people fled in fear and panic. But 'Amr ﷺ was seen in the front ranks, jumping on his healthy foot and shouting, "I desire Paradise, I desire Paradise!" His son Khallad ﷺ was behind him. Both father and son remained fighting until they fell in the battlefield, taking the rank of martyr, *Shahid*, only a few minutes apart.

In this battle, 'Amr's brother-in-law was also martyred. When Hind ﷺ received the news of the martyrdom of her husband, her son and her brother, she first asked after the welfare of the Prophet ﷺ. When they told her he was well, she went to him and said, "If you are safe, all calamities are reduced to nothing."

Then she had all three bodies of her family members placed on a camel, and she began to direct it towards Madinah. On the way, she met one of the wives of Rasulullah ﷺ, 'A'ishah ﷺ, who was going with other women to look after the Prophet ﷺ. Hind ﷺ was able to tell her that Rasulullah ﷺ was alive and not severely injured. Then she told her that here on the camel were the bodies of her husband, son and brother who had all been martyred in the battle.

At that instant, the camel, as if it had heard her, sat down and would not budge. No matter what they did, it would not move. 'A'ishah ﷺ thought perhaps the camel was overloaded, but Hind ﷺ explained that it was used to carrying more than this. At last they gave up, raised the camel and turned toward 'Uhud. The camel stood and walked willingly. Hind ﷺ carried all the three bodies to Rasulullah ﷺ. He asked her whether any of them had said anything while leaving the house. Hind ﷺ said that on leaving the house, her husband had prayed, "O Allah, bless me with martyrdom; do not send me back to my family with my hopes dashed!"

As he looked at 'Amr ﷺ lying in the sand, he ﷺ said, "When certain slaves of Allah swear for a certain purpose, Allah fulfills their desire. 'Amr is among such slaves. I witness that he is walking here and there in Paradise and his lame leg is set right."

Rasulullah ﷺ ordered that all the the martyrs of 'Uhud be buried at the site of the battle without washing. He said to his companions, "Leave them with their blood and wounds - I am their witness. Any Muslim wounded for the sake of Allah will come on the Day of Judgment with his blood running, its color like saffron (deep gold) and its smell like musk (the best of scents)." He added,

"Bury 'Amr ibn al-Jamuh with 'Abdullah ibn 'Amr, as they were sincere friends."

This is why the camel turned around.

It is said that six months later, 'Abdullah ibn 'Amr's son ﷺ excavated the grave to shift his father's body to some other place. The bodies of both the friends were found as fresh as the day they were buried.

May Allah ﷻ bless 'Amr ibn al-Jamuh, his family and his friends, martyrs of Uhud.
May their graves be illuminated.

'Ikrimah ibn Abi Jahl

*"'Ikrimah will come to you as believer and emigrant.
Don't insult his father. Insulting a dead man hurts who
is alive and does not reach the dead."*
Muhammad Rasulullah ﷺ

"**W**elcome to the emigrant traveler,"
the Prophet ﷺ greeted 'Ikrimah
one day.

Rasulullah ﷺ greeted 'Ikrimah warmly on
this day, but many long and difficult years had
passed for both of them before this friendly
meeting.

'Ikrimah was twenty-eight years old when
Rasulullah ﷺ made his mission public. 'Ikrimah's
lineage was one of the most noble of the Quraish,
and he belonged to one of the wealthiest families.

His father, the notorious Abu Jahl, was a very strong influence on 'Ikrimah. Allah ﷻ tested the faith of the believers through the torments of 'Ikrimah's father, and the believers remained firm in spite of him. Abu Jahl tormented, chased, insulted and killed the Muslims at every opportunity and without conscience.

'Ikrimah, under his father's influence, developed the toughest opposition to the Prophet ﷺ. Like his father, he tortured the Muslims as much as he could, carrying out his father's wishes, which he made his own.

Abu Jahl led the armies of the Quraish to the Battle of Badr. He prepared for the battle by slaughtering camels, drinking wine and listening to the music of singing girls. On the day of Badr itself, Abu Jahl was the leader and 'Ikrimah was his right hand man.

When he was leaving for Badr, Abu Jahl had sworn by the goddesses Lat and 'Uzza that he would not return alive to Makkah unless he defeated the army of Rasulullah ﷺ. But Lat and 'Uzza were only idols with no real power, and so his prayer to them was useless. Abu Jahl was killed in that battle and his son witnesed him being killed.

'Ikrimah had to return to Makkah, leaving his father's corpse behind. The defeat prevented him from taking it for burial in Makkah. Because he fled with the other Makkans, the body was left with the Muslims who threw it into al-Qalib, the mass grave where all the *kuffar* killed at Badr were buried. There lay the corpse of Abu Jahl, under the sand, and no one among the Muslims was sad to know it was there.

From that day, 'Ikrimah adopted a new attitude toward Islam. At first he had fought Islam for the sake of his father, and now he did so for the sake of revenge. 'Ikrimah and others whose relatives were killed at Badr kept feeding the flame of hatred in their hearts. They encouraged the desire for revenge which led eventually to the Battle of 'Uhud.

The Need For Revenge

'Ikrimah ibn Abi Jahl went to 'Uhud, and he took with him his wife Umm Hakim to be with the other Quraishi women whose relatives were slain at Badr. They stood behind the lines beating drums and urging the warriors to fight, so that no one would think of running away.

Khalid ibn al-Walid led the right flank of the Quraishi army, and 'Ikrimah led the left flank. These two warriors led the Quraish to victory that day over the Muslims. Abu Sufyan ibn Harb, the

Quraish chief, said, "This is for the day of Badr!" They felt they had gotten their revenge against the Muslims.

At the Battle of al-Khandaq (the Trench), the Quraish besieged Madinah. They were stopped by the trench which no one could cross. It was a long siege and 'Ikrimah grew impatient. He looked for some place in the ditch that was narrow enough to leap and raced his horse towards it. He managed to cross and was followed by a few others. One of them was killed and 'Ikrimah had to turn and jump back across to save himself.

On the day of the conquest of Makkah, the Quraish knew they could not stand up to the Muslims any longer. They decided to let Rasulullah ﷺ enter unopposed. This decision was made easy for them since they knew that Rasulullah ﷺ had given instructions to his commanders to fight only if someone of Quraish attacked them first.

However, 'Ikrimah and some others went against the consensus of Quraish. They attempted to block the progress of the Muslim forces. Khalid ibn al-Walid ☺, who had become a Muslim and had gone over to the army of the Prophet ﷺ, defeated them in a small battle. Some were killed and the others fled. Among those who escaped was 'Ikrimah.

At that point, 'Ikrimah was desperate. After

Makkah surrendered to the Muslims, its people shunned him. The Prophet ﷺ had granted a general pardon to all Quraish with the exception of a very few whom he named and ordered to be killed, "even if they were found under the curtains of the *Ka'bah*." At the top of that list of names was 'Ikrimah ibn Abi Jahl.

So he slipped out of Makkah, disguised, and headed south towards Yemen, since he had no other refuge.

The Day of Welcome

'Ikrimah's wife, Umm Hakim, along with Hind bint 'Utbah and ten other Makkan women, went to the house of the Prophet ﷺ to pledge allegiance to him. When they found him, he was sitting with two of his wives, his daughter Fatimah and a number of other women of the clan of 'Abd al-Muttalib ﷺ. Hind was fearful of meeting Rasulullah ﷺ, because of the way she had mutilated the body of his uncle, Hamzah, at the Battle of 'Uhud. She was so afraid that she came in his presence wearing a veil over her face.

She said, "O Rasulullah ﷺ, praise be to Allah Who has established the religion He chose for Himself. I implore you by the bonds of kinship to treat me with mercy. I am now a believing woman." Then she unveiled her face and said, "I am Hind bint 'Utbah."

"You are welcome here Hind," replied the Prophet ﷺ.

Then she said, "O Rasulullah ﷺ, by Allah, there was no house on earth that I wanted to see disgraced more than your house. Now there is no house on earth that I would like to see honored more than your house."

Then, Umm Hakim stood up and declared her entrance into Islam and said, "O Rasulullah, 'Ikrimah ran away from you to Yemen out of fear that you would kill him. Grant him security and may Allah grant it to you."

"He is secure," promised the Prophet ﷺ.

There were three men left who had fought fiercely and tirelessly against Rasulullah ﷺ. They were 'Ikrimah, Safwan, and Suhail. The Prophet ﷺ gave each one security for a period of time, and eventually they all embraced Islam. 'Ikrimah was the first.

Umm Hakim set out immediately in search of her husband. She traveled south along the coastal road until she found 'Ikrimah at Tihamah on the Red Sea, trying to arrange transport to Ethiopia with a Muslim seaman. The seaman was saying,

"Be honest with Allah and I will transport you."

"What shall I say?" asked 'Ikrimah.

"Say: *'I testify that there is no god but Allah!'*" was the answer, for the captain feared shipwreck if he took an unbeliever aboard.

"I have run here to escape from these words!" said 'Ikrimah. At that moment, he realized that he actually could say those words that he had resisted all his life. He also knew that since he could say them, there was no need to get on the boat to run away from saying them. Then Umm Hakim ﷺ arrived and said, "O husband, I have come from the most generous of men, the most righteous, the best - Muhammad ibn 'Abdullah ﷺ. I asked him to grant you security and he did. Don't destroy youself by running away farther."

"Have you really talked to him?" asked 'Ikrimah.

"Yes, I have, and he has granted you pardon!"

She kept reassuring him until he agreed to come back with her. At a rest house on the way, he wanted to sleep with her, but she refused absolutely and said, "I am a Muslim woman and you are a *Mushrik,* an idol-worshipper."

'Ikrimah was totally amazed that his wife would refuse him and he said, "Any matter that comes between us, keeping you from me, must be a great matter!"

As 'Ikrimah approached Makkah, Rasulullah ﷺ said to his companions, "Ikrimah ibn Abi Jahl will come to you as a believer and emigrant. Don't insult his father. Insulting the dead hurts the one who is alive and does not reach the dead."

Soon after that, 'Ikrimah and his wife arrived at the place where the Prophet ﷺ was sitting. When Rasulullah ﷺ saw him, he stood up and greeted him without even putting his cloak on, as he normally would have. His face was full of welcome.

When the Prophet ﷺ sat down again, 'Ikrimah said, "O Muhammad, Umm Hakim told me you have granted me pardon."

"She said the truth," said the Prophet ﷺ. "You are safe."

"What do you invite people to, Muhammad?" asked 'Ikrimah.

Rasulullah ﷺ said, "I invite you to testify that there is no god but Allah and that I am His Messenger, to make the *Salah* and to pay *Zakah*..." and the Prophet ﷺ went on explaining the pillars of Islam.

'Ikrimah responded, "I swear you are inviting only to the Truth, and you are commanding only to do what is good. You lived among us before you started your mission. You were the most honest and the most righteous of us." Then he stuck out his hand and said, "I testify that there is no god but Allah and that you are His servant and His Messenger and...O Rasulullah, teach me the best thing to say!"

"Say: I testify that there is no god but Allah and that Muhammad is His servant and His messenger." "Then what?" asked 'Ikrimah.

"Then say: I call on Allah and those who are present to witness that I am a Muslim, a *Mujahid* (one who fights for Allah only), and a *Muhajir* (an emigrant for Allah)." And 'Ikrimah ﷺ said so.

At that point the Prophet ﷺ said, "Whatever you ask me today, I will give you."

'Ikrimah ﷺ said, "I ask you to ask Allah's forgiveness for me for all the hatred I had against you, for all the moments I confronted you and for whatever I said in your presence or absence."

Rasulullah ﷺ responded, "O Allah, forgive him all the hatred he had against me, wherever he went intending to put out Your Light, and whatever he said insulting me in my presence or my absence." 'Ikrimah's ﷺ face beamed with happiness and he said, "By Allah, O Rasulullah, I promise that whatever I have spent to obstruct the way of Allah, I shall spend twice as much for His sake, and whatever fight I have fought against the way of Allah, I shall fight twice as hard in His way."

Fighting For Allah

From that day on, the ranks of Islam gained a brave horseman in the fields of battle and a great worshipper who spent his nights praying and his days reading the Qur'an in the *Masajid*.

'Ikrimah ﷺ fulfilled his promise to Rasulullah ﷺ, giving the Muslims more than he had spent against them, and fighting very hard in the way of Allah ﷻ. In fact, he took part in every battle or expedition that took place after he became Muslim. Years later, 'Ikrimah ﷺ marched into Palestine with the Muslim armies. At the decisive Battle of Yarmuk, 'Ikrimah ﷺ plunged into the fight like a thirsty man who finds cold water on a hot day. When the attack grew heavy on the Muslims, 'Ikrimah ﷺ left his horse, broke his sword's scabbard and charged deep into the ranks of the Byzantines. His old companion Khalid ibn al-Walid ﷺ rushed to him and said, "Don't! Your death would be too hard on the Muslims!"

"Leave me alone, Khalid," answered 'Ikrimah ﷺ. "You had, in the past, an honorable relationship with Rasulullah, but my father and I were his bitterest enemies. Let me make up for what I have done in the past. I fought Rasulullah on many occasions - shall I flee now from these Byzantines? This shall never be!"

Then, calling out to the Muslims, he shouted, "Who will pledge to fight until death?" Four hundred responded to his call. Among them was his uncle Harith ibn Hisham, and also Dirar ibn al-Azwar and 'Ayyash ibn Abi Rabi'ah. They fought heroically and bravely and protected the position of their leader Khalid 🕮.

When at last the Byzantine army was routed and the Muslims assured victory, the bodies of three mortally wounded warriors were lying on the earth of Yarmuk: Harith ibn Hisham, 'Ayyash ibn Abi Rabi'ah and 'Ikrimah 🕮. Even in their moments of death, they exhibited the generosity toward one another that had characterized the *Sahabah*. Harith 🕮 asked for some water to drink. As it was brought to him, 'Ikrimah 🕮 looked at him, so Harith 🕮 said, "Give it to him."

When they brought the water to 'Ikrimah 🕮, 'Ayyash 🕮 looked at him, so 'Ikrimah 🕮 said, "No, give it to him." By the time they got to 'Ayyash 🕮, he had just breathed his last. When they returned to Harith and 'Ikrimah 🕮, they found that they too had passed away.

May Allah 🕮 bless them all and give them a drink from the waters of al-Kawthar, the pool in Jannah, so they'll never be thirsty again, and may He grant them the green fields of the highest paradise (Firdaws).

Nu'aim ibn Mas'ud

"Say what you want to draw them off,
for part of war is trickery."
Muhammad Rasulullah ﷺ

N u'aim ibn Mas'ud lived in the desert region of central Arabia called the Najd. He had sharp wits and a perceptive heart. He was very intelligent and possessed many admirable qualities: acute intuition, swift responses and keen shrewdness. Such qualities are developed when a man has to be a quick thinker to stay alive in the desert, and has to follow his intuition to find food and companionship. But Nu'aim had a weakness. He was a pleasure-seeker. He loved music and drinking and would go to Yathrib to seek these things.

Nu'aim was willing to travel all the way to

the oasis town of Yathrib when he became tired of the sand, heat and emptiness of Najd. Each time he longed for music, he went to the Jewish villages around Yathrib. The Jewish tribes were well known for their accomplishments in the arts and Nu'aim paid their musicians generously. Over time, he developed close ties with the Jewish tribes of the oasis, and he became especially connected with the Banu Quraizah.

Denying the Truth

While moving back and forth between Yathrib and the Najd, Nu'aim got word of some strange and mysterious changes taking place in the city of Makkah. He heard that a man there had proclaimed himself a prophet of Allah and was calling people to quit the worship of idols. He heard other things about this prophet's new teachings as well, many of which did not please him. He heard that this man was calling for polite and generous treatment of women and love and tenderness to the lower classes. These things he didn't mind.

But this new prophet was also calling for a general passing over of selfish pleasure in favor of helping others in need. The fun-loving Nu'aim was definitely not interested in such austerities. He was used to indulging in pleasures whenever his heart desired, and did not want to give up this freedom. Nu'aim was more concerned with what he could see right in front of him. He began to develop a negative impression of Islam out of fear that it would come between him and his enjoyment.

Because of his bad impressions, Nu'aim chose to befriend the harshest enemies of Islam. He fought in the army the Banu Ghatafan against the Muslims. He allied himself with the Quraish in Makkah. And he sided with the Jewish tribes of Khaibar. Nu'aim had even been to Madinah to try to trick many Muslims whose faith was weak to surrender. He had been paid by the Quraishi chief, Abu Sufyan ibn Harb, to convince the Muslims that it was useless to continue fighting. But while he was spreading rumors in Madinah, he witnessed the power that Islam had in peoples' lives. A tiny seed of faith took root in his heart which was to blossom later.

The Jews of the Banu Nadir tribe in Madinah had broken their treaty of peace and protection with Rasulullah ﷺ. They violated the terms of the contract very clearly - they had attempted to have the Prophet ﷺ assassinated. Many Muslims thought they should be executed, but the Prophet ﷺ, in his mercy, simply ordered them to leave Madinah. The Banu Nadir left Madinah with their families and all they could carry, in a great caravan, and headed north. Many of them settled in the oasis of Khaibar. There, they plotted and planned revenge. They started to put together an alliance to fight the Prophet 🌸 and wipe out the growing influence of Islam.

The Banu Nadir went to the Quraish and urged them to march once more against Madinah. They promised the Quraish that they would help them by providing them with weapons and money. By fueling their anger, they helped to kindle the fires of hatred and make the Makkans more eager for a new battle.

The Banu Nadir told Abu Sufyan ibn Harb, "We are one with you against the trouble-maker Muhammad!"

Abu Sufyan replied, "The dearest of men to us are the ones who will help us against that man!"

So Abu Sufyan ibn Harb and the other Quraishi chiefs took the Banu Nadir inside the *Ka'bah* and they all swore an oath that they would stick together in their goal to destroy Islam. Abu Sufyan then asked them, "Men of the Jews, you are the people of the Torah, and you are a people of knowledge. We want to know: is our religion of many gods better, or is that of Muhammad?"

The chiefs of the Banu Nadir answered, "Your religion of many gods is better than his, and you are nearer to the truth than he is." Of course they knew it wasn't. But they knowingly lied against their own Torah in order to keep good relations with the idol-worshippers. Both groups then agreed on a date to meet in secret outside Madinah.

Then the Banu Nadir went to the tribe of Banu Ghatafan in Najd to rally them against the Prophet ﷺ. They called them to come and destroy the Muslims. They offered them the same promise of money, weapons, and men. The Banu Nadir also offered them half the date harvest of Madinah. Once the Banu Ghatafan were convinced, they too agreed upon the the date for the secret meeting.

The Quraish, with their warriors, horses, and camels, left Makkah under the leadership of their chief, Abu Sufyan ibn Harb, and headed for Madinah. At the same time, a small group of Muslims secretly left Makkah to warn the Prophet ﷺ.

Also at the same time, the Banu Ghatafan left Najd. They were fully equipped for war, with 2,000 men under the command of 'Uyainah ibn Hiln. And in the front rank of this force was Nu'aim ibn Mas'ud.

Allied Against Islam

As the various armies set out on their mission, the small group of Muslims from Makkah reached Madinah. They warned Rasulullah ﷺ of the coming danger, and they estimated that the Muslims had only a week to prepare their defenses. Rasulullah ﷺ gathered his *Sahabah* to discuss plans for war. They had to make a decision about how to defend themselves.

Madinah had never faced such a huge army before; nearly 10,000 men were in the united force of the *Ahzab*, the "Allies," including the Quraish, the Banu Nadir and Banu Ghatafan. If the Muslims went out of the city to fight, they would be overwhelmed by sheer numbers. And if they stayed in the city, the invaders could attack and endanger the lives of their families. The Muslims were at a loss at what to do.

But soon an interesting proposal came from Salman al-Farisi ﷺ. He told them about a strategy that was used by the people in his native Persia. This was to dig a great trench around the city. No one in Arabia had ever heard of such a thing before, but the Muslims decided to try it. It seemed the best way to confront the huge army, without endangering the security of their families and the rest of Madinah. Work began on digging the trench.

74

The men worked without stopping alongside Rasulullah ﷺ, and the trench was dug in six days. It was completed just in time. The Muslims then spread their men out along it, one man about every five or six feet, and they had just enough men to go around. The trench stretched in an arc around Madinah, leaving open only the side that was facing the strong fortresses of the last remaining Jewish tribe of the city, the Banu Quraizah. This was the only Jewish tribe to have kept its treaty with the Muslims. Now the Muslims had to rely on them to stay loyal against their own people coming from outside. It was a dangerous situation.

The armies of the *Ahzab* met on the plain outside the city, ready to attack. As they rode forward, they were greatly surprised to find themselves confronting not the Muslim army drawn up for battle, but a deep trench in the ground which they could not cross. They were furious and started calling the Muslims cowards, saying that this was not the "Arab" way to do battle. They had to camp in front of the trench, because they could not attack the city.

Day after day the enemy warriors rode out and tried to cross or leap the trench. And day after day they were driven back by the arrows and spears of the Muslims. The *Ahzab* couldn't get close enough to cross, and the Muslims couldn't get close enough to hit them either. So the armies just stayed facing each other. Still, they were close enough to feel the constant tension and danger.

In the meantime, the Jewish leaders of the Banu Nadir went to the fortresses of the Banu Quraizah on the other side of Madinah. They urged them to join the Allies in fighting the Muslims.

The chiefs of the Banu Quraizah said to them, "You're asking us to do what we really would prefer to, but you know that we have taken a treaty with Muhammad so that we can live peacefully here in Madinah. You also know that this treaty is still valid, and we are afraid to break it. We fear that if Muhammad wins this war, he might expel us from Madinah in return for our betrayal."

But the agents from the Banu Nadir persisted in urging them to break their promise to Rasulullah ﷺ and betray the Muslims. They kept assuring them that this time there was no way the Muslims could win since several great armies were attacking at once. They promised the Banu Quraizah that they could have anything they wanted in Madinah when the Muslims were defeated. They reminded them how nice it would be if they could have Madinah all to themselves, with all of its fortresses and orchards.

Eventually, the Banu Quraizah accepted these bribes and broke their promise to the Prophet ﷺ.

They tore their written agreement apart and declared they were joining the *Ahzab* in their war against him. This news hit the Muslims like a thunderbolt.

The Prophet's Du'a

Soon, the armies of the *Ahzab* surrounded Madinah and deprived it of all supplies. Their horses and camels ate up all the gardens and grass around the city. Their tents were spread all over the plain outside Madinah, and their campfires at night seemed to stretch for miles. Their soldiers harassed the Muslims all day long, threatening to jump the trench, shooting arrows here and there, and shouting insults so that the Muslims could get no rest. The Muslims felt themselves in a terrible position, with the Quraish and the Banu Ghatafan camping before them outside the city and the Banu Quraizah behind them inside the front lines.

Then the *Munafiqun*, the hypocrites, started saying what was hidden in their hearts: "Muhammad used to promise us the treasures of Khusraw and Heraclius. Now we are not even safe going outside our own homes!"

They started to desert Rasulullah ﷺ in groups. They complained that they feared for their women, children, and houses, because the Banu Quraizah would attack them when the war started in earnest. Rasulullah ﷺ ended up with only a few hundred *Mu'minun*, true believers, to defend the whole city.

The siege dragged on and on. Everyone was exhausted. Food supplies were running very low and no one could get more than a few hours' sleep at a time. The weather was terribly cold and bitter. The *Ahzab* were unhappy, but they had many replacements and could at least sleep.

But the Muslims were physically worn down. They could only keep going because of their faith and the presence of Rasulullah ﷺ, who held them together and kept them firm. Every night, warriors rode through the city shouting, *"Allahu Akbar! Allahu Akbar!"* to encourage the people who were not on the trench and to frighten the hypocrites and the Banu Quraizah so that they kept out of mischief.

One night Rasulullah ﷺ took refuge with Allah ﷻ and kept making the *Du'a' al-Mudtarr* (the prayer of the one who has no other recourse), repeating: *"O Allah, I beg You to fulfill Your oath and Your promise...O Allah, I ask You to fulfill Your oath and Your promise..."*

That night, Nu'aim ibn Mas'ud was lying at the entrance of his tent. He was having a sleepless night and felt as if his eyelids were fixed open with nails. He kept gazing to the sky, following the floating stars...he kept thinking and wondering. Suddenly he started thinking to himself:

Shame on you, Nu'aim! What brings you so far away from Najd to fight this man and his friends? You aren't fighting him for revenge. He has never hurt you. He has never dishonored you. You are a clever and intelligent man. Why on earth would you risk killing or, worse, getting killed, for no reason?

Shame on you, Nu'aim! This good Muhammad teaches his followers justice, generosity, and goodness.

You have seen how they fight so courageously, never giving up. Look at them, holding out against this huge force.

You fool, why would you drive your spear into his companions who follow the guidance he brought to them?

Nu'aim cut off his thoughts by jumping up from his mat, wrapping himself up in his cloak, and taking a quick walk to rectify his thoughts.

He sneaked out of the camp in the darkness. Very carefully, he slipped across the trench and, crouching like a moving shadow against the ground, made his way to Rasulullah ﷺ.

The Prophet ﷺ was standing alone, making

Du'a'. When he saw this man suddenly standing before him, he said calmly, "Nu'aim ibn Mas'ud?"

"Yes, Mesenger of Allah."

"What brings you here?"

"I come," said Nu'aim, "to testify that there is no deity but Allah and that you are His servant and messenger and that what you brought is true...O Prophet, command me to do whatever you want. My people do not know anything about my Islam."

Rasulullah ﷺ had the ability to bring out the best in people, and utilize their talent for the most benefit. He knew the negotiating talents of Nu'aim ibn Mas'ud ﷺ, and he also knew that Nu'aim ﷺ was a very clever man.

The Prophet ﷺ said, "Staying with us, you are just one more man. You can help most if you go back to your people and try to set the different tribes against each other."

Nu'aim ﷺ asked permission to spread confusion in the ranks of the *Ahzab*.

Rasulullah ﷺ told him, "Say what you need to divide them, for part of war is trickery."

Planting the Seeds of Mistrust

Nu'aim ibn Mas'ud ﷺ crept through the city and went straight to the Banu Quraizah. They welcomed their old friend and offered him food and drink.

He thanked them but said, "O Banu Quraizah, you know my affection for you and my honesty in giving you advice." They agreed that he had always been helpful and reliable.

So Nu'aim ﷺ said, "I fear for your safety and have come to warn you and give you advice."

"What do you know?" they asked.

"You can see that the Quraish and the Banu Ghatafan are in a different position than yours. You are here in your own homes. It is here that you have all of your money, your children and your women. You cannot leave this place for another. You have nowhere to run. The Quraish and Banu Ghatafan, on the other hand, have their land, their money, their children and their women far away from here. They came to fight Muhammad. Their friends, the Banu Nadir, asked you to break your treaty and your promises to support them. And you agreed.

"If the *Ahzab* win, both you and they will benefit from the victory. But if they fail, they will return safely to their homes. They will leave you to the mercy of the Muslims. And surely Muhammad will not be too happy with you. You know very well you truly can't afford to fight in this war."

"You're right," said the chiefs of the Banu Quraizah, "What do you think we should do?"

Nu'aim 🙵 advised the Banu Quraizah to ask the *Ahzab* for some of their noblemen as hostage. If they agreed to this, it would show the truthfulness of the intentions of the *Ahzab*. He told the Banu Quraizah that they should not do anything for the *Ahzab* unless they agreed to give hostages.

"This would force them to fight Muhammad with you until victory," said Nu'aim, "or until the last man dies, because they won't be willing to leave their hostages without help."

The chiefs of the Banu Quraizah had been afraid of this possibility, that the *Ahzab* might just get fed up and leave. They thought this hostage idea was very good advice. Before he left, Nu'aim 🙵 got them to promise that they wouldn't tell the *Ahzab* who had given them the idea.

Nu'aim 🙵 left them and went quietly back to his own tent on the other side of the trench. Then he went to his old friend Abu Sufyan ibn Harb, chief of the Quraish. He told Abu Sufyan he had some very important news to share, but could only relate it on condition that they swear they would tell nobody from whom they heard it. They all swore they would tell no one.

"O Quraish, you know my love for you and my hatred of Muhammad. I have received some news and I think it is really your right to know, if I am to be loyal to you. But you must keep this to yourselves and never reveal that I'm the source.

"You know I have some old relations with the Banu Quraizah. I've now found out that they regret breaking their treaty with Muhammad. They think he might win this war. They have sent him a message saying that they feel sorry for what they did and that they have decided to return to the terms of their peace treaty with him. They asked him if he would be satisfied if they took some of the nobles of Quraish and Ghatafan and hand them over so the Muslims can cut off their heads. Muhammad has agreed to their proposal. So if the Banu Quraizah send you a messenger asking for hostages, don't give them any!"

Abu Sufyan, deeply shocked, said, "What a good friend you are Nu'aim! May you be rewarded."

Then Nu'aim 🕮 left Abu Sufyan and the Quraish and went to the leaders of Ghatafan. He told them what he had just told Abu Sufyan and warned them as he had warned him.

In order to be sure that Nu'aim's 🕮 news was actually true, Abu Sufyan wanted to test the Banu Quraizah and see if he could somehow confirm what he had been told. He sent his son to them.

His son told the Banu Quraizah, "My father

sends you his greetings and says to you: 'Our siege of Muhammad has lasted too long, and we have decided to finish him off once and for all. We are going to attack tomorrow, so prepare for battle.'"

They said to him, "Tomorrow is the *Sabbath*. We Jews don't do any work on the *Sabbath*. And we won't fight with you at all until you give us seventy nobles of yours and Ghatafan's as hostages. We fear that you may return to your homes if the battle goes against you, and leave us to face Muhammad on our own. You know we couldn't survive that!"

When Abu Sufyan's son returned to his people and told them what he had just heard from Banu Quraizah, they said all together, "Shame on the sons of Banu Quraizah! Nu'aim ibn Mas'ud was telling us the truth. If they now ask us for a sheep as a hostage we wouldn't give it to them!"

Nu'aim ibn Mas'ud ﷺ succeeded in sowing so much distrust in the ranks of the *Ahzab* that they lost their unity. They were already dissatisfied in any case. Their horses kept getting shot with arrows, some of the camels were even dying, they were running out of food and there was no plunder in sight. Only the Quraish and the Banu Nadir had any real fight with Muhammad ﷺ; the others from Najd had just hoped for the plunder of Madinah.

Allah ﷺ then sent a terrible hurricane upon

the Quraish and their allies. It tore their tents apart, put out all their fires, turned over their cooking pots, threw sand in their faces and clogged their eyes and noses with dust. Huddled on the ground, they felt themselves attacked by more than the wind. They felt that Muhammad ﷺ, whoever he was, had help from the Unseen.

They had no other choice but to leave for home. They left, in the darkness of the night.

When the morning came, and the dim light of dawn, the Muslims found that the enemies of Allah ﷻ had all run away. They praised Allah ﷻ and they hugged one another, as they felt enormous relief. Rasulullah ﷺ gave them all permission to return to their homes.

An Honest and Faithful Follower

From that day on, Nu'aim ibn Mas'ud ﷺ remained a true follower of Rasulullah ﷺ. He took on responsibilities and duties, and he helped to bring many of his tribe members into Islam.

On the day of the opening of Makkah, Abu Sufyan ibn Harb stood looking at the Muslim armies as they marched past. He saw a man carrying the standard of Banu Ghatafan. He asked who the man was and when he was told that it was Nu'aim ibn Mas'ud ﷺ, he said,

"How bad was what he did to us the Day of the Trench. By Allah, he was once the worst enemy of Muhammad and here he is carrying his people's standard!"

Allah ﷻ had transformed a pleasure-seeker into a warrior, and a trickster into a truthful leader of men.

May Allah ﷻ reward him for his sacrifice and surrender to the Truth of Allah ﷻ.

Nu'man ibn Muqarrin al-Muzani

"And of the wandering Arabs there is he who believes in Allah and the Last Day, and takes that which he expends for offerings, bringing him near to Allah and the prayers of the Messenger. Surely it is an acceptable offering for them. Allah will bring them into His mercy. Lo! Allah is All-Forgiving, Merciful."
Surah at-Tawbah, verse 99

Near Madinah, along the road that led to Makkah, lived a tribe called the Banu Muzainah. They were always in contact with those who traveled the road, and they would listen to the stories and news that these travelers brought. Naturally, they had come to hear of Rasulullah ﷺ and of his *Hijrah* to Madinah. Everything they heard made them think well of the Prophet ﷺ and of Islam.

The leader of this tribe, Nu'man ibn Muqarrin, was a thoughtful man and always tried to keep the best interests of his people as a priority. One night, he was sitting in an expansive black tent with his relatives and other notables of his tribe. He said, "O my people, by Allah, we know only good things about Muhammad. We have heard that he teaches mercy, goodness and fairness to all those who will listen. Why do we delay in going to meet him? We sit here next to Madinah, while other people are rushing to him from great distances."

He fell silent, and then continued, "I have decided to go to him tomorrow. Whoever wants to come with me should prepare for the journey."

It seemed as if his people were just waiting for this guidance from their leader. When Nu'man arose in the morning, he found his ten brothers and four hundred people of the Banu Muzainah prepared to go with him to Madinah to meet Rasulullah ﷺ.

This was a large number of people and although Nu'man was pleased, he was also ashamed to go to Rasulullah ﷺ without taking gifts to him.

But they had a problem. Since this was a

year of drought, the Banu Muzainah had no money or food left. In fact, they had barely enough to eat for themselves. Nu'man searched among his belongings and those of his brothers, since they were the leaders of their tribe. He found and gathered a few sheep that the drought had spared.

The people of Madinah may have been alarmed at seeing such a huge number of people descending on their city. This alarm soon changed to joy when the Banu Muzainah informed them they had come to see the Prophet 攀. They went and in front of him 攀 they all declared their Islam.

This was a momentous day in Madinah. It was certainly the first time so many people had become Muslim at once. And it was the first time eleven brothers had pledged their love to the Prophet 攀 all together! The day was also blessed because Allah 攀 sent down a revelation through Angel Jibril 攀 to Rasulullah 攀, in which He told of His acceptance of the poor thin sheep and the people who presented them as a gift:

"And of the nomadic Arabs there is he who believes in Allah and the Last Day, and takes that which he expends for offerings, bringing him near to Allah and the prayers of the Messenger. Surely it is an acceptable offering for them. Allah will bring them into His mercy. Lo! Allah is All-Forgiving, Merciful."

The chief Nu'man 🕮 put himself willingly under the leadership of Rasulullah 🕮, and participated in all the battles against the unbelievers. He and his people fully embraced Islam, and dedicated themselves completely to its cause.

Loyal Supporters of Islam

Years later, after the death of Rasulullah 🕮, many of the desert tribes tried to get out of paying the *Zakah* and began to move away from Islam. But Nu'man 🕮 and the Banu Muzainah remained firmly committed to their Faith. Their attitude had a great effect on other tribes, and helped in putting an end to the rebellion during the *Khilafah* of Abu Bakr as-Siddiq 🕮.

During the *Khilafah* of 'Umar ibn al-Khattab 🕮, military campaigns continued. But now they were not with the rebellious tribes of the desert. Rather, they were with the Persians and the Byzantines. Nu'man 🕮 was sent with the Muslim army that marched into Sasanid Iraq.

The commader of the Muslim forces was Sa'd ibn Abi Waqqas 🕮. After many clashes with the Sasanid Persians, he was preparing for a major confrontation. Following the practice, or *Sunnah*, of Rasulullah 🕮, he sent a delegation to the Sasanid

Shah, Yazdigird. The purpose of this delegation was to invite the *Shah* to Islam. For this task, Sa'd ﷺ appointed Nu'man ﷺ.

They reached al-Mada'in, the capital of the Sasanid Empire, and asked to be introduced to the *Shah*. They were well received in his audience chamber, which was very grand. The *Shah* asked for a translator and through him he asked the Muslims, "What tempted you to make war on us? Maybe you dared do such a thing because of the fact that we are busy with other matters?"

Nu'man ﷺ turned to his companions. He said, "Let me answer the *Shah*. If any of you wants to speak after me, so be it." His companions agreed. They turned to the *Shah* and said that Nu'man ﷺ was going to speak for them.

An-Nu'man ﷺ thanked Allah ﷻ and praised Him, asked for blessings on His Prophet ﷺ, and then addressed the ruler of all of Persia, saying, "Allah ﷻ has granted us mercy by sending a Messenger who guides us to goodness and commands us to follow it. That glorious man is he who shows us what is evil and forbids us to follow it.

"He promised us that Allah ﷻ will give us the good of both this world and the next. After we answered the call of this man, Allah exchanged our poverty for wealth, our humiliation for dignity, and our enmity for mercy and brotherhood. Our Prophet ﷺ then commanded us to call people to what is best for them and to start with our neighbors.

"So, we are inviting you, O great king, to enter Islam. It is a Way that approves all that is good and encourages it and a Way that resents all kinds of ugliness and warns against it. It takes its followers from the darkness and injustice of the ego to the light and justice of true faith.

"If you respond to the invitation of Islam, we will leave the book of Allah with you, leaving to you the responsibility of ruling according to its regulations. We will turn back and leave you alone and Allah will surely make you a righteous king.

"However, if you reject the Way of the Messenger for Mankind ﷺ, we will take tribute from you and protect your lives and property.

"But if you refuse to do even this, we shall assuredly fight you."

The *Shah* was a proud ruler with immense power. Hearing this final threat he burst into a rage. Furiously, he said to the Muslims, "I know no people on earth who are as miserable as you Arabs! We used to let the governors of our most desolate provinces take care of you and make you obey us!"

The *Shah* calmed down a little and continued, "Look, if it is poverty that pushed you to come to us, we will order food for you until your land becomes fertile again. We will send silken garments for your leaders and we will assign a governor who will take good care of you."

At this offer, one man from the Muslim delegation replied to the *Shah* in a way that made the *Shah* angry again.

So *Shah* Yazdigird said, "Were it not bad manners for diplomats to be killed, I would have you all beheaded. Get out of my sight! I have nothing for you. Tell your chief that I am sending my army to bury him and all of you Arabs who dare to cross me!"

Then he asked for a bag of dirt and said to his courtesans, "Let the most noble of these Arabs carry this dirt until he exits from the gates of the capital of my kingdom."

So they asked the Muslim delegation, "Who is the most noble-born among you?" 'Asim ibn 'Umar said, "I am," as he was the son of the current *Khalifah*, 'Umar ibn al-Khattab ⬥.

So they gave him the bag of dirt and he carried it until he left al-Mada'in. Then 'Asim ⬥ put it on his camel and took it to Sa'd ibn Abi Waqqas ⬥, bringing him the good news that Allah ⬥ would grant the Muslims the conquest of Persia and would make them possessors of everything from gold to the soil of its land.

Eventually, a huge battle took place between the Muslims and the Sasanid Persians in Iraq, at a place called Qadisiyyah. But it was Yazdigird's army that was buried by the Muslims, not the Muslims' army as Yazdigird had so foolishly boasted.

Leader of the Muslim Army

Though the Sasanids had a terrible defeat at Qadisiyyah, they were still persistent and powerful. Instead of completely losing hope after this battle, they pulled back and regrouped their armies.

When the news of a new Sasanid army reached the *Khalifah* 'Umar 🕮, he decided to confront this great peril himself. But some of the notable Muslims convinced him to give up that plan, as he was needed in Madinah. They urged him to send someone in place of him, who would be a reliable and strong leader.

'Umar 🕮 asked them for their advice on whom to appoint as leader. "You know better than we do, *Amir al-Mu'minin,*" they replied.

"By Allah," said 'Umar 🕮, "I'll assign this responsibility to a man who, when both parties meet, is faster than their swords: Nu'man ibn Muqarrin al-Muzani." And everyone agreed to the choice.

So 'Umar 🙏 wrote to Nu'man 🙏, saying:

From the slave of Allah, 'Umar ibn al-Khattab, to Nu'man ibn Muqarrin. News has reached me of the huge number of Persians who are gathering before you in a place called Nahawand. Whenever this letter reaches you, go with the soldiers who are with you but do not hurt your men by pushing them through rough mountain roads. One Muslim is worth more to me than one hundred thousand *Dinars*. May Peace be with You!

Nu'man 🙏 led his army to meet the enemy deep in Persian territory. He sent scouts out to explore the countryside. When the scouts got close to Nahawand, their horses stopped. Although they tried to push them, the beasts didn't move. Curious as to why the horses refused to move, they examined their animals to find sharp iron nails in their horses' hooves. They looked on the ground and discovered that the Sasanids had sprinkled these things all over the road to Nahawand to hinder any enemy from reaching it. The Persians had many tactics like this, and they used them to their advantage.

The horsemen returned to their army, and told Nu'man 🙏 what they had discovered. They asked for his advice. He commanded them first to stop where they were and to set many campfires in the night for the enemy to see, to make it obvious to the Persians that they were there. He told them that after they had done this, they should pretend to be afraid and defeated, thus tempting the Persians to pursue them and to remove the iron thorns they had sprinkled with their own hands.

The plan worked. As soon as the Sasanid Persians saw the first batches of the Muslim soldiers pretending to retreat, they sent their men to pick up the spikes so that they could pursue. But as soon as these spikes were removed, the Muslims turned and charged right into the Sasanid ranks! With this attack the Muslims were able to take control of the road.

Nu'man ﷺ camped with his army on the outskirts of Nahawand. He planned to surprise the enemy with an attack. He said to his soldiers, "I will make *Takbir* (*"Allahu Akbar"*) three times. On the first one everyone should get ready, on the second everyone should tie his weapon to his body, and on the third, we will assault the enemy!"

Nu'man ﷺ made his *Takbir* three times. He said, *"Allahu Akbar!"* and everybody tightened up. He said, *"Allahu Akbar!"* and the soldiers tied their weapons to their bodies so they would not drop them in the heat of battle. Then he cried, *"Allahu*

Akbar!" and plunged into the Persian ranks, the Muslim soldiers flowing after him in a torrent. Perhaps in the whole of human history, there has never been an attack as ferocious as that day!

The Sasanid army was torn apart; the bodies of their men filled the valley and covered the mountainsides. Nu'man's ﷺ horse slipped on the blood of the slain and Nu'man ﷺ was crushed to death under its weight. One of his brothers took the battle flag from Nu'man's ﷺ hand and covered him with a cloak. Fearing the Muslims would lose heart if they found out their general had died, the brother hid the news.

When victory at Nahawand was complete, the victorious, exhausted and blood-stained Muslim warriors asked about their brave leader. His brother then removed the cover and said, "Here is your leader. Allah has delighted him with victory and ended his life with martyrdom."

Thus Nu'man's brother ﷺ, who had embraced Islam at the same time as he, carried on the family heritage of honor and self-sacrifice. As 'Abdullah ibn Mas'ud ﷺ once said about them, "There are houses of faith and of hypocrisy. The house of Nu'man is one of the houses of faith."

May Allah ﷺ be pleased with Nu'man ibn Muqarrin al-Muzani and his family ﷺ. Amin.

98

Salman al-Farisi

"Salman belongs to us. He is of my Ahl al-Bait, my Family."
The Messenger of Allah ﷺ

*T*he account of how Salman al-Farisi, *the Persian*, came to Islam is one of the greatest conversion stories in history. He would become one of the most beloved men to the Prophet ﷺ and his contributions to the Muslim *Ummah* are numerous. This is how Salman ﷺ related his story of finding the Truth:

I was a young Persian from Isfahan, from a village called Jayy. My father was the lord of the village. He was the richest man, and the noblest. From the time I was born, I was the most beloved son of my father. His love for me was very strong. As time passed, he feared losing me so much that he confined me to home

99

as if I were a prisoner.

I became devoted to the Zoroastrian faith of our ancestors. I became responsible for taking care of our family's sacred fire, and it was my duty to keep it burning so that it would not go out for a single minute, day or night.

Now my father owned a large farm that brought in a lot of money. He looked after it himself. One day, he was too busy to go to the farm to check on things, so he said, "O my son, as you can see, I am too busy to go to our farm. You have to go today and take care of it." He gave me certain instructions and then said, "Don't let yourself be late, because you are more important to me than my farm, and worrying about you will prevent me from going about my business!"

So I started out, heading for the farm. On my way, I passed by a Christian monastery, and the sound of the singing from within attracted my attention. I didn't know anything about it because my father kept me in the house away from people. When I heard the voices, I entered into the yard of this monastery to find out what they were doing.

I was impressed by the prayer of the monks there and felt drawn to their worship. I said to myself, "This is much better than what we Zoroastrians do!" So I stayed with the monks until the sun set and I did not go to my father's farm. I asked them where this religion came from and I was told it originated in Syria.

At night I returned home. My father had been so worried that all his work had been interrupted. He asked me where I had been, and why I hadn't followed his instructions. I said, "O Father, I saw people praying in a monastery. I was curious and stayed with them until sunset."

My father was horrified and exclaimed, "There is no good in their religion, son! Our ancestral faith is better!"

"No father," I answered, "their religion is better than ours!"

My father feared that I would leave our faith, so he tied me up and imprisoned me in the house again. When I got the opportunity, I sent a message to the Christian monks, saying, "Whenever a caravan comes from Syria, let me know."

Soon after, they sent me word that a caravan had indeed arrived. I asked the monks to see if the merchants would take me back to Syria with them when they finished their business. They agreed to do this.

I managed to untie my legs and escaped from the house. I joined that caravan in disguise and accompanied them to Syria. There, I asked the people who was the most learned person in their religion. They said, "The bishop of the main church."

I went straight to this bishop and said, "I want to become Christian. I would like to serve you, to learn from you and to pray with you."

"Come in," replied the bishop and I entered the church and stayed in his service. However, I soon found out that the man was corrupt. He would order his followers to give money for charity, tempting them with the blessings they would receive. But when he was given money to be spent in the way of God, he would treasure it for himself and never give a poor man any of it. Thus he filled seven huge jars with gold. I hated him very much for that.

After a while, this bishop died and the Christians gathered to bury him. But I came out and told them that he was a hypocrite and that he used to gather money for charity from them and kept it for himself, never giving any of it to the poor.

"How can you possibly know this?" they exclaimed.

"I will show you his treasure," I replied. They agreed to follow, and I took them to where he hid the seven huge jars filled with gold and silver. When they saw that they said, "By God, we won't bury him!" They put him on a cross and threw stones at him. Then they appointed someone else in his place.

I continued my service with the new bishop. I have never seen any non-Muslim whom I consider more ascetic, more devoted to the next world, and more conscientious night and day in his worship than he. I loved him more than I had ever loved anyone. I stuck to him as long as he lived.

When he was very close to death, I told him how much I loved him and I asked him to name someone whom I could follow after him. He said, "O my dear son, I don't know anyone like me. Men have died and have changed or left most of their true faith, except for one man. He lives in the Iraqi town of Mosul. So go and find him."

When the bishop died, I went to Mosul, found the man and told him my story. He was very good, just as my late bishop had described. I stayed with him but it was not long before he lay dying. Before he died, I asked him to tell me whom I could follow and he advised me to find a certain man in a village called Nasibin. This man was as good as the first two had been. I followed him until he died. Then I went to

'Ammuriyyah to meet another man whom [the man from Nasibin] had advised me to follow. I stuck to that man, who was as good as the others. There I worked until I earned some cows and a few sheep.

Before he too died, I asked him to advise me what to do and whom to follow. He said, "O son, by God, I don't know anyone on earth who follows what we have followed anymore. But the time has come for a prophet to appear in the land of the Arabs. He will be sent with the message that was given to Abraham. After a time he will migrate from his city to another city that has plenty of palm trees between two areas of black lava rocks. He will have obvious signs [by which you can recognize him]: he will eat what is given, but he won't eat what is given in charity, and between his shoulders there is the Seal of Prophecy. If you can reach his land, then try to do so. For with him is salvation and a clear path to our Lord God."

This Christian holy man died and was buried. I stayed in 'Ammuriyyah until a group of Arab merchants arrived. I asked them to take me to Arabia in exchange for my cows and sheep. They agreed, and took me with them in exchange for my animals. But when we reached Wadi al-Qura (a valley between Madinah and

Syria), they betrayed me and sold me to a Jew as a slave.

I worked as a servant. As there were many palm trees in the area, I hoped this would be the place that had been described to me by my teacher, but I was not sure. Then a cousin of my master came from the Banu Quraizah of Madinah and bought me and took me with him back to his town. As we approached the town, I saw the palm trees that my friend of 'Ammuriyyah had told me about. I saw the black lava rocks on either side. I knew it was the city he had described to me and I lived there in hopes of the coming of the new prophet.

By that time, Rasulullah ﷺ was in Makkah inviting his people to Islam. But I did not hear anything about him since I was so busy with my duties as a slave. When the Prophet ﷺ reached Madinah after his *Hijrah*, I was on top of a palm tree belonging to my master, while he was sitting under the tree. A cousin of his came to him and said, "May God kill the tribes of the Aws and Khazraj. They are all gathered at Quba, waiting for a man from Makkah who claims to be a prophet of God!"

As soon as I heard what he said, I felt as if I were in a dream and I started to shake and tremble so much that I was afraid I was going to fall on my master. I climbed down quickly and said to the man, "What did you say? What did you say?"

My master got angry at my questions and gave me a terrible blow on the ears. Then he said, "This does not concern you slave! Go back to what you were doing!"

When the evening came, I took some dates I had gathered and went to where Rasulullah ﷺ was staying in the village of Quba. I said to him, "I heard that you are a virtuous man. You and your *Sahabah* are strangers here and are in need. Here is some charity; I thought you deserve it more than others," and I gave the dates to him.

The Prophet ﷺ offered the dates to his companions, but he didn't hold out his hand, and he didn't eat them himself. I told myself, "That's the first!" and I left.

When Rasulullah ﷺ left Quba for Madinah, I gathered more dates and went to him and said, "I noticed you don't eat food given as charity but these dates are a present which I freely give you." So he ate the dates and offered some to his companions and they all ate together. I told myself, "That's the second!"

Many days later, I went to Rasulullah ﷺ as he was burying one of the *Sahabah* in a piece of land that would later be known as *Jannat al-Baqi*. He was sitting with a cloak over his shoulders. I greeted him and began to look on his back for the seal my friend of 'Ammuriyyah had described. When the Prophet ﷺ noticed I was looking at his back, he knew what I was looking for and threw back his cloak. When I saw the seal, I burst into tears and started kissing him.

"Come to me," said the Prophet ﷺ. So I came and sat before him and told him my story. He wanted his *Sahabah* to hear it as well.

Obtaining Freedom

Salman ﷺ had finally found that great prophet foretold in the Bible. But after that miraculous meeting, he had to return to his work as a slave. He found very little time to be with the Prophet ﷺ. This must have been very hard for him, for because of this he was unable to fight at Badr or 'Uhud. He had spent many years of his life trying to find Rasulullah ﷺ, and now that he had found him, he could not be with him.

While he was discussing this problem one day, the Prophet ﷺ said to him, "Write a contract." So Salman ﷺ wrote to his master saying he wanted to buy his freedom. To pay for it he would plant three hundred palm trees, digging out the holes, and, in addition, he would pay 20 ounces of gold.

Rasulullah ﷺ called on his *Sahabah* to help Salman ﷺ. They helped, one with thirty little palms, another with twenty, another with fifteen, and another with ten, each helping as much as he could until the three hundred saplings were gathered. Then the Prophet ﷺ told Salman ﷺ to start digging holes for them. When he had finished, the Prophet ﷺ put each of the saplings in with his own blessed hands. Some of the Companions helped Salman ﷺ dig and when they had completed all the holes they went to Rasulullah ﷺ. One by one they brought the palm shoots and he ﷺ planted them himself. By Allah ﷻ, not one of these plants died.

So the palm trees were delivered, but Salman ﷺ still owed his master the gold. The Prophet ﷺ had been given a piece of gold from a mine and it was the size of a hen's egg. He told Salman ﷺ to take it and pay off his freedom with it. But Salman ﷺ knew it wouldn't cover the price of the agreed amount. He asked the Prophet ﷺ how much of his debt it would pay. The Prophet ﷺ took the gold and turned it over on his tongue.

"Take it," he said to Salman ﷺ, "for Allah will buy your freedom with it."

So Salman ﷺ took it to his master and

weighed it out for him. The gold piece weighed exactly 20 ounces. Thus, Salman ﷺ was able to pay his debt with it and was free.

The Brilliant Proposal

Salman ﷺ was freed right before the Battle of the Trench. When the Muslims learned of the huge force that was marching against them, they met to decide how to defend the city. And it was Salman ﷺ who suggested that they dig a trench around it, as this was a kind of defense used in the large empires of the north with which he was familiar. No one in Arabia had ever used this type of tactic before.

The Muslims completed the trench in six days, just before the enemy arrived. When the *Ahzab* tried to attack, they found that they could neither jump over nor climb across the trench. Their plans were completely frustrated.

There are many stories about the digging of the trench. Rasulullah ﷺ worked alongside his *Sahabah*, and whenever they hit a really difficult rock or hard place in the earth, they would call him. Salman ﷺ relates:

I was working with a pick in the trench when a rock began to give me a lot of trouble.

The Prophet ﷺ, who was nearby, saw me hacking away at it and saw how difficult the place was. Dropping down into the trench, he took the pick from my hands. He gave the rock such a blow that sparks came flying out from beneath the pick. A second and a third time he struck, and each time I saw a flash of sparks going off in a different direction. When the rock broke, I asked him, "O you who are dearer to me than my own soul, what is the meaning of that light coming from your strikes?"

He said, "Did you really see that, Salman? The first means that Allah has opened up Yemen to me. The second means that Allah has opened Syria and the West. The third means that Allah has opened the East."

And all of those places were soon opened and I saw them opened in my lifetime.

On the day that Salman ﷺ proposed to dig the trench for the Battle of the Trench, all of the Muslims were very proud of him. Since Salman ﷺ had no tribe, all the Arabs wanted to adopt him. The *Muhajirun* claimed that he was one of them. He had, indeed, made a *Hijrah*. Likewise the *Ansar* said he was theirs, since he was living in Madinah when the Prophet ﷺ came.

But Rasulullah ﷺ took him and said, "Salman

belongs to us, the *Ahl al-Bait* (the People of the House of Rasulullah ﷺ).”

Rasulullah ﷺ also praised Salman ﷜ saying “Paradise longs for three: for 'Ali, 'Ammar bin Yasir, and Salman al-Farisi.”

May Allah ﷻ bless Salman al-Farisi ﷜
for the day he began looking for the Truth
everywhere, the day he found the Truth
and believed sincerely in it, the day he died,
and the day he will be resurrected.

112

Suhaib ibn Sinan ar-Rumi

"The selling has achieved its benefit, Abu Yahya, the selling has achieved its benefit."
Muhammad ar-Rasulullah ﷺ

Despite his name, Suhaib ar-Rumi ﷺ was not truly a Roman but a pure Arab. His father was from Banu Numair and his mother from Banu Tamim. However, he spent many years of his life in the Byzantine Middle East, learning the language and culture, which was Greek and Roman in origin. When he returned to Arabia, he carried with him experiences that would be useful knowledge for the Muslims.

Twenty years before Rasulullah ﷺ began receiving revelations, a tribal chief named Sinan ibn Malik an-Numairi was ruling al-Uballah, which was an important city in southern Iraq. The area was

113

controlled at that time by the Sasanid Persians, and Sinan, being an Arab, was ruling as governor for the emperor at that time, *Shah* Khusraw.

The most beloved son of Sinan was a boy named Suhaib. Suhaib ﷺ had fair skin, blond hair, and an active, intelligent personality. He was a very joyful child, full of light, and he brought a great deal of happiness to his father, who was often burdened by the difficulties of governing.

One day, Suhaib's ﷺ mother left for a short vacation to a village in central Iraq. She took her son with her. Allah ﷻ had written for them an incident that would change their lives forever. A company of Byzantine cavalry raided this particular village, killed its menfolk, robbed its treasury, and captured all the children. Suhaib ﷺ was among the captives.

Taken away from his mother and everything familiar, he was sold in the slave market in Byzantium. Suhaib had to serve many masters, like thousands of other slaves in Byzantium.

Due to his low status, Suhaib ﷺ had no privacy and he was not able to make his own choices in life. Being intelligent, however, he took the opportunity to learn all about Byzantine society, and to know it from the inside.

By that time in history, the Byzantine empire had become corrupt. There was a great deal of injustice and unfairness in every aspect of life. Many people (especially those from the ruling class) did not take their Christian religion seriously, and they used to violate many of its values. He witnessed life in the palaces with his own eyes, which was full of backbiting and plotting, and he heard with his own ears the injustice and wickedness of the nobles. He hated their way of life. He used to tell himself: "A society like this can only be purified by a flood like that of Noah ﷺ."

While in Byzantium, Suhaib nearly forgot his Arabic language. He never spent any time with Arabs and was raised in the Byzantine province of Anatolia (modern-day Turkey), among people who spoke Greek. But he never forgot his roots among the Arabs.

Escape to Freedom

Suhaib ﷺ longed for the day he could escape. He yearned to be free and to rejoin his people. One day, he heard a Christian priest telling one of his masters, "I believe we are close to the time when a prophet will appear in Makkah, in Arabia. He will affirm the message of Jesus son of Mary ﷺ and he will lead people from darkness into light." Suhaib ﷺ listened carefully and wondered to himself if this coming prophet might change the way of life of the Byzantines to a much more godly and better one.

When the opportunity finally came, Suhaib ﷺ ran away from his masters and headed for Makkah, in the land of the Arabs, where the prophet was expected to appear. When he arrived there and settled in the village, the Arabs began to call him Suhaib ar-Rumi, the Roman, because of his foreign accent and his red hair.

As a "foreigner," Suhaib ﷺ needed someone to do business with in Makkah. He became partners with one of the leading traders of the city and carried out business which earned him a great deal of money. His hard work and his gift of working well with people helped him to have a prosperous business.

Nevertheless, Suhaib's ﷺ business activities did not make him forget the comments of that Christian priest. He used to wonder when that prophet would reveal himself. Sadly, Suhaib saw in Makkah many of the same injustices he had experienced among the Byzantines. He felt that the whole world needed a change.

Finding the Truth

One day, Suhaib ﷺ was returning to Makkah with one of his caravans when he was told by someone that Muhammad ibn 'Abdullah ﷺ was telling people that he was sent by Allah ﷻ, and that he had started calling people to believe in one God, urging fairness and goodness and warning against evil. Muhammad ﷺ was telling the Arabs to leave their old ways and their old pagan religion.

Suhaib ﷺ commented, "Isn't he the one they call *al-Amin*, the Honest?"

"Yes," was the reply. Everyone knew about the honesty of Muhammad ﷺ.

"Where is he now?" asked Suhaib ﷺ.

He was told that the Prophet ﷺ could be found in the house of al-Arqam ibn Abi al-Arqam near the hill of Safa. "But watch out that no one of Quraish notices you," they warned, "because if they see you they will do bad things to you; you are only a foreigner with no clan to protect you."

Suhaib ﷺ went cautiously to the house of Arqam. When he arrived there he found 'Ammar ibn Yasir ﷺ at the door. Since he already knew him, he went up to him with some hesitation and said, "What are you doing here, 'Ammar?"

"You too should be asked that," replied 'Ammar ﷺ.

"I want to see that man and hear what he says," said Suhaib ﷺ.

"Me too," said 'Ammar ﷺ.

"So let's enter together with the blessing of

Allah," replied Suhaib ﷺ.

Suhaib and 'Ammar ibn Yasir ﷺ went in to see Rasulullah ﷺ and listened to what he said. The light of his presence awakened their faith, and they felt as if they had found what they had always been looking for. Without waiting another day, they took his hand and testified that there is no god but Allah ﷻ and that Muhammad ﷺ is his slave and messenger.

They spent the whole day with him, learning from him and enjoying his company. At last, when night came and the regular noises of the day calmed down, they left, hiding in the dark, each one carrying in his chest enough light to enlighten the whole world.

Suhaib ﷺ endured his share of torture along with dozens of other Muslims ﷺ. Because he was a foreigner he had an especially hard time, but he withstood the tortures and insults and refused to leave the faith he had found at last. He knew from the teachings of his beloved Prophet ﷺ that the road to Heaven is surrounded by hateful things. Suhaib ﷺ suffered this hard life for many years.

Yet Suhaib ﷺ kept making money. He was a very good businessman, and if he couldn't make money with the Quraish, he would do business with travelers or with the Syrians or Jews. He became very rich.

The Best Exchange

When Rasulullah ﷺ at last gave permission for the Makkan Muslims to emigrate to Madinah, Suhaib رضي الله عنه decided to accompany the Prophet ﷺ and Abu Bakr رضي الله عنه on their trip. But the men of Quraish figured out his decision to go and stopped him. They assigned guards to watch Suhaib رضي الله عنه so that he might not run away, taking with him all the gold and wealth he had earned in trade.

After Rasulullah ﷺ made the *Hijrah* with Abu Bakr رضي الله عنه, Suhaib رضي الله عنه kept waiting for an opportunity to join them, but it was all in vain. He couldn't go anywhere without being watched. So Suhaib رضي الله عنه had no choice but to use a trick.

One cold night, Suhaib رضي الله عنه repeatedly went out of his house as if he had to go to the bathroom. He hardly came in that he went back once more. The guards said to each other with a laugh, "Don't worry, Lat and 'Uzza have kept him busy with his stomach so he won't get far!" And with that, they all went to sleep. Suhaib رضي الله عنه then slipped away and headed for Madinah.

Soon after he was gone, the guards woke up and realized he had escaped. They raced their horses until they caught up with him. When Suhaib رضي الله عنه heard the thunder of hooves, he climbed up a hill, took his arrows out of their quiver, strung his bow and waited.

When they caught up with him and stopped their horses just out of range of his arrows, he said to them, "O Quraish, you know I am among the best and most accurate archers. By Allah, you will not reach me before I kill one of you with each arrow I shoot. Then, I will strike you with my sword for as long as I can keep it in my hand."

One of them replied, "By god, we will not let you and your gold go. When you came to Makkah, you were just a homeless wretch. It was there [in our city] where you got your riches!"

"That is true! So if I leave you my money," said Suhaib 🕮, "would you let me go?"

"Yes," they answered without any hesitation.

So Suhaib 🕮 told them where he had hidden the money in his house. Some of them went back and found the money. They took it, returned and allowed him to go.

Suhaib 🕮 rushed to Madinah, escaping with nothing except his faith. He didn't feel sorry giving up the gold he had spent his life gathering. Each time he felt exhausted from the trip, he remembered he was going to Rasulullah 🕮. When he thought of this, he felt his energy coming back and he went on through the desert.

When he reached the village of Quba, the Prophet 🕮 saw him coming. He was very pleased and said to Suhaib ⟨⟩, who was also known as Abu Yahya, "The selling has achieved its benefit, Abu Yahya, the selling has achieved its benefit."

Suhaib ⟨⟩ beamed with happiness and exclaimed, "By Allah, no one got here before me with the news. None but Jibril ⟨⟩ could have told you."

The selling of Suhaib ⟨⟩ had indeed achieved its benefit. It was approved by a revelation from Allah ⟨⟩. Jibril ⟨⟩ witnessed it, and the following verse descended about Suhaib ⟨⟩:

And of humankind is he who would sell himself,
seeking the pleasure of Allah; and Allah has
compassion on his slaves.
(al-Baqarah 2:207)

May Suhaib ibn Sinan ar-Rumi ⟨⟩ have
bought himself the Jannah when he left Makkah,
and may he rest with the Mercy of his Lord.

121

Suraqah ibn Malik

"How would you feel, Suraqah, if you wore both of Khusraw's bracelets?"
Muhammad Rasulullah ﷺ

T he Quraish could not believe that the Blessed Prophet ﷺ had slipped away from Makkah. Had not seven men been stationed to guard his house, to kill him in the morning? Seven men from each of the great families, surrounding him, awake and watching? Yet somehow he ﷺ had come out the door and walked past them without one of them seeing him.

How? All night, they had guarded the figure wrapped in a cloak who slept within the home of Rasulullah ﷺ. In the beginning of the night, this figure had indeed been that of Rasulullah ﷺ. But at dawn, they had seen the figure rise from his bed and come to the door. It was 'Ali ﷺ, not Muhammad ﷺ! How? Where was the Prophet ﷺ? They had searched his house, and had found only the women. As the news of his escape spread throughout the city, the chiefs of Quraish hurried to their meeting place near the *Ka'bah*. They had to act quickly, for they knew his destination - Madinah. They knew his purpose as well - to establish an authority that they would never accept. They knew what they must do - stop Islam before it gained a firm foothold. They wanted the Prophet ﷺ, dead or alive.

The Makkans searched for him in every neighborhood of the Banu Hashim, the Prophet's ﷺ own clan. And they searched the houses of his *Sahabah* ﷺ, though many of their houses were now abandoned, their occupants moved to Madinah.

Certain Arabs were famous for their ability to track in the desert. By the slightest of signs - a broken twig, a blurred footprint, a disturbance in the dust - they could determine the direction taken by a camel, horse or a man. These trackers were now lured by a huge reward offered to search for Rasulullah ﷺ. The Quraishi chiefs offered 100 camels to the one who could find the Prophet ﷺ.

Unknown to them, Rasulullah ﷺ and Abu

Bakr ﷺ had actually taken a path toward the south. They were hiding in a cave on a deserted hillside. The two had determined to wait there until the excitement among the Quraish died down and travel became safer.

The *kuffar* were coming closer and closer. "By god, your man is in this cave!" the guide said to the other five men. They all stopped just outside the lip of the cave to look around.

Umayyah ibn Khalaf answered sarcastically, "Don't you see the spider web on its door? It's older than the birth of Muhammad! And those birds that flew away just as we arrived - do you think they would be nesting outside a cave with men in it? Don't be a stupid fool!" So they went back down the mountain.

The Search Continues

The Quraish leaders didn't stop their search for Rasulullah ﷺ. They continued to spread the word to all the tribes that they were eager to have him, and that the reward for his capture would be more than generous.

Suraqah ibn Malik al-Mudlaji was sitting in a meeting with his people in a small village near Makkah, when a messenger from the Quraish came in. He announced the news of the great prize for whoever found and captured the Prophet ﷺ.

As soon as Suraqah heard about the hundred camels, he determined to join the manhunt. But he controlled himself and didn't whisper a single word, so that others wouldn't be tempted to do the same.

One of the people of his tribe said, "By Allah, three men just passed by me going in such-and-such a direction and I think they are Muhammad, Abu Bakr and their guide."

Suraqah however, told him, "No, no! they are so-and-so, looking for their lost camel."

"Maybe," said the man and he fell silent.

Suraqah remained sitting quietly for a while, so as not to arouse anyone's interest. But in his head he was busy making plans. When the people started talking about something else, he slipped away and went home. He ordered his servant to prepare his horse and bring it up from the valley where it was grazing. He asked for his weapons and they were brought.

Taking with him a little food and a canteen, he armed himself. He took along his divining arrows, which the pagan Arabs used in those days to "foresee the future." Mounting his horse, he rode off swiftly in the direction described by the man at the meeting.

Suraqah was one of the best horsemen

among his people. He was tall, athletic and quite talented in tracking. He was also a clever poet who composed verses for himself as he rode along. His horse was a thoroughbred Arabian that rode like the wind and had never failed him yet.

In later years, Suraqah 🙼 narrated the events as follows:

> When I cast the divining arrows, out came the arrow which I did not want: *"Do him no harm."* I did the same again, and again the arrow which I did not want came out: *"Do him no harm."* I was dearly hoping to bring him back to the Quraish so that I might win the reward of a hundred camels.
>
> So I rode in pursuit of him anyway and when my horse was going at a good pace it stumbled and threw me. I thought this was somewhat unusual so I used the divining arrows again and out came the detestable, *"Do him no harm."*
>
> But I refused to be put off and rode in pursuit. Again my horse stumbled and threw me, and again I tried the arrows. They told me, *"Do him no harm."*
>
> I rode on, and at last, as I finally saw the three men, my horse stumbled and I fell. Then, as it got its legs up, smoke arose like a

sandstorm. When I saw this smoke I knew that he was protected against me and would have the upper hand.

I called to them, saying I was Suraqah ibn Malik and asked them to wait for me. I shouted that they need not worry, for no harm would come to them from me.

The Prophet ﷺ told Abu Bakr to ask what I wanted and I said, "I know now that no one can defeat you. Write a document for me which will be a contract between you and me." And the Prophet ﷺ instructed Abu Bakr to do so.

Abu Bakr ﷺ wrote on a piece of leather and threw it to me and I put it in my quiver. They were about to ride off, when the Prophet ﷺ said to me, "How would you feel, Suraqah, if you were to wear Khusraw's two bracelets?"

"Who? Khusraw son of Hormuz?" asked Suraqah. "The great king of Persia?"

"Yes," replied Rasulullah ﷺ, "Khusraw son of Hormuz." And they rode off.

Puzzled by such strange words, Suraqah ﷺ returned home and people came to him seeking news. He said to them all, "Go back to your homes! I searched everywhere. You know how accurate my tracking is. It's not worth your trouble."

He kept the matter of Rasulullah ﷺ secret

and didn't tell his story until he was sure that they had reached Madinah and were out of danger.

Time passed, years went by, and Suraqah ﷺ lived his life in the desert like so many other Arabs. But he never forgot the little piece of writing that he kept in his quiver. At last the day came when Rasulullah ﷺ returned to Makkah a great conqueror, with 10,000 warriors, armed and shouting in one voice, *"Allahu Akbar! Allahu Akbar!"*

Those who had offered a hundred camels for his life (or rather, those of them still left alive) were terrified. "What do you think I am going to do to you?" asked the Noble Messenger ﷺ from the door of the Ka'bah.

"You are a noble and generous man, the son of a noble and generous man," his former enemies cried, expecting the worst. "We can do nothing! You may do as you will!"

But the Messenger ﷺ answered in the words of the Qur'an,

Allah forgives you, and He is the most
Merciful of the merciful.
(*Yusuf* 12:92)

Soon after that, the Muslims fought in the Battle of Hunain and then laid siege to the town of Ta'if. On the road to Ta'if, Suraqah met the Muslim army. Holding the leather parchment in his hand, he forced his way through the ranks of the *Ansar* cavalry. They became annoyed and tried to move him away saying, "Off with you! What do you want? This is no place for interlopers! This is an army!" But Suraqah kept pushing through until he reached the side of Rasulullah 襲, who was mounted on a camel.

Suraqah 襲 lifted his hand that was holding the leather note, and said, "O Rasulullah, I am Suraqah ibn Malik! This is your written promise to me, from that day I tried to capture you and your companion many years ago."

The Prophet 襲 said, "This is a day of repaying and goodness. Come near, Suraqah."

Suraqah 襲 relates, "I approached him and took Islam from him 襲. Then I remembered something that I wanted to ask him. All I can remember now is that I said, 'Stray camels used to come to my fountain which I kept full for my own camels. Will I get a reward for letting the strays have water too?'

"'Yes,' he said, 'for watering every thirsty creature there is a reward.'"

A short while after Suraqah 襲 met Rasulullah 襲 this second time, the Noble Messenger 襲 passed into the next world. Suraqah 襲 felt deep sorrow at the death of Rasulullah 襲.

He kept recalling the day that he tried to kill Rasulullah ﷺ for a mere hundred camels. Suraqah ؓ knew now that all the camels in the world did not equal even the dust beneath the sandals of Rasulullah ﷺ.

Suraqah ؓ kept thinking about his words, "How would you feel if you were to wear Khusraw's two bracelets?"

Suraqah ؓ had no doubt that he was indeed going to wear them one day.

The Promise Fulfilled

After some years, 'Umar ibn al-Khattab ؓ became *Khalifah* of the Muslims. By that time, nearly all the Arab tribes had embraced Islam and the Muslim armies were engaged in conflict with the Byzantine and Sasanid empires.

After many harsh and horrible battles, the Muslims had nearly overcome the Sasanids. With the help of the conquered people themselves, the Muslims were able to overcome fortresses, capture castles and occupy towns. Then, at last, the capital city of the Sasanids in Iraq, al-Mada'in, fell.

One day, towards the end of 'Umar's ؓ *Khilafah*, messengers from Sa'd ibn Abi Waqqas ؓ came to Madinah bringing the good news of victory. They also brought along with them one-fifth of the treasure they had obtained during their war against the Sasanids. This they brought to be deposited into the Muslim treasury.

When the treasure was put before 'Umar ﷺ, he was stunned, as were all those who were with him. They had all heard of the riches of the Sasanid *Shahs*. But for the Arabs, who had borne such hardship and had lived with so little for so long, seeing these riches laid out in front of them was truly amazing.

The treasure included Khusraw's crown, bedecked with pearls, his clothes embroidered with golden thread, his shawl beset with jewels and his two matchless bracelets.

'Umar ﷺ had a stick in his hand, and with it he kept turning over pieces of this precious treasure. Then he turned to the people around him and said, "Those who brought these treasures are surely honest people!"

'Ali ibn Abi Talib ﷺ, who was there, said, "You have been honest 'Umar and so have your subjects. Had you been corrupted, your subjects would have been corrupted too."

Then 'Umar ﷺ called Suraqah ﷺ and put on him *Shah* Khusraw's shirt, trousers, shawl and slippers.

He girded him with the imperial sword and belt. He put the *Shah's* crown on his head, and both the royal bracelets in his wrists. When they saw the two bracelets, the Muslims could stand it no longer and began to shout: *"Allahu Akbar! Masha'Allah!"* because everyone knew of what the Prophet ﷺ had told Suraqah ؓ many years before. His meeting with Rasulullah ﷺ had been the greatest event in his life and he never got tired of describing it to anyone who would listen.

'Umar ؓ looked at Suraqah ؓ and said, *"Masha'Allah!* A little Arab from the desert, from the Banu Madlaj, with Khusraw's crown on his head and his two bracelets on his wrists!"

Then he lifted his head to the heavens and prayed:

O Allah, You kept this wealth from Rasulullah ﷺ, who was more cherished and honored by You than anbody.

You kept it from Abu Bakr who was more cherished and honored by You than we are.

You gave it to me, so I take refuge with You from giving it to me...

Before he left the meeting, he had already distributed it among the Muslims.

May Allah ﷻ compensate Suraqah for his generosity - in Heaven. Amin.

134

Thumamah ibn Athal

*"This is a man who at the beginning of the day
ate with an unbeliever's stomach
and at the end of the day with a Muslim's."*
Muhammad Rasulullah ﷺ

In the sixth year of the *Hijrah*, Rasulullah ﷺ began to extend the call to Islam beyond Makkah and Madinah. He sent eight letters to Arab chiefs and foreign kings, inviting them to Islam. One of these rulers was Thumamah ibn Athal al-Hanafiyyah. Thumamah was one of the most powerful rulers in those days. He was a noble from among the greatest nobles of the Banu Hanifah tribe and a chief of al-Yamamah. He commanded the loyalty of many people.

The people of Yamamah were economically

powerful because they produced excess grain. After the people had taken what they needed, there was still more to be sold. They were the chief suppliers of grain to Makkah, and the Makkans depended upon them for a steady supply of food, because they themselves had no land that could be cultivated. Thumamah ibn Athal was a prominent grain merchant, and he had very strong contacts with the traders of Makkah.

When Thumamah received the Prophet's ﷺ letter of invitation, he took it with contempt and rejected it. He refused to listen to this invitation to truth and goodness. Not only did he refuse to listen to the beautiful message of Islam, he even began to formulate a way to strike out against the Muslims.

One day, Thumamah captured 'Ala ibn Abdullah Hadhrami ؓ, a well-known companion of Rasulullah ﷺ, who happened to be passing through the region. Thumamah was bent on killing 'Ala ؓ. But by the grace of Allah ﷻ, Thumamah's uncle, 'Amir, who was a good-natured person, came to the rescue and prevented the execution. 'Ala ؓ later described the event to Rasulullah ﷺ, who prayed for the welfare of 'Amir and said about Thumamah, "O Allah! Put Thumamah under my control!"

Not long after that, Thumamah ibn Athal decided to make *Umrah*. He left al-Yamamah and headed for Makkah, intending to make *Tawaf* around the Ka`bah and to make sacrifices to its idols.

The Gentle Imprisonment

When Thumamah had reached a place near Madinah, on his way to Makkah, something happened that he was not expecting. A troop of Muslim warriors was patrolling the outlying areas out of fear that some stranger might cause trouble. This troop captured Thumamah without knowing who he was, took him back to Madinah, and tied him to one of the columns of the *Masjid an-Nabawi*, waiting for Rasulullah ﷺ himself to decide what should be done with him.

When Rasulullah ﷺ came into the *Masjid*, he saw Thumamah tied to the column, and said quietly to his guards, "Do you know whom you have captured?"

"No we don't, Rasulullah," they replied.

He said, "This is the chief Thumamah ibn Athal al-Hanafi, so treat him well."

The Prophet ﷺ went back home and asked for all the food they had to be sent to Thumamah. Then he ordered his she-camel to be milked for Thumamah twice a day. All this happened before Rasulullah ﷺ had even gone to speak to Thumamah.

Rasulullah ﷺ came to Thumamah, who was still tied to the pillar inside the *Masjid*, hoping to encourage him to become Muslim. "What do you have to say, Thumamah?" he asked.

Thumamah replied, "O Muhammad, if you kill me, you kill one whose blood must be paid for. If you want a ransom, ask what you like."

The Prophet ﷺ left Thumamah two more days just as he was. But he continued to be politely taken care of, having his food and milk served to him. During this time he observed and heard everything that went on in the *Masjid an-Nabawi*. Finally, Rasulullah ﷺ came back to him and said, "What do you say, Thumamah?"

Thumamah replied, "Enough, Muhammad. If you kill me, you kill one whose blood must be paid for; if you want a ransom, ask what you like."

The Prophet ﷺ left him till the next day, then came to him asking, "What do you say, Thumamah?" and Thumamah repeated the same reply. So Rasulullah ﷺ turned to his companions and said, "Set him free," and they did.

Thumamah left the *Masjid an-Nabawi* and rode until he reached *al-Baqi*, a place that later became a cemetery for many of the *Sahabah*. This place had a well, so he knelt his camel down, washed himself, and returned back to the *Masjid*. When he got there he stood before a group of

Muslims and said, "I witness that there is no god but Allah and I witness that Muhammad is His messenger." Then he said to Rasulullah ﷺ:

"O Muhammad, by God, there was never on this earth a face more detestable than yours. Now, yours is the dearest face of all to me. By Allah! Earlier than this moment, no Way, no *Din* was as abominable as this Islam, but now no Way is better than this Way. By Allah! I hated no town as much as Madinah, but now this city appears to me the most beautiful on earth. O Messenger of Allah, I left my land intending to perform *'Umrah*. Now this has happened in the course of my journey and Allah has blessed me with the faith of Islam. Can I now perform the *'Umrah?*"

Rasulullah ﷺ replied, "If there is no danger to your life in Makkah, go ahead and perform your *'Umrah*, but it must be in accord with the way of Allah, not that of the idol-worshippers." Then he taught Thumamah ﷺ how to perform *'Umrah* in the correct way.

Thumamah ﷺ was relieved and said, "By Allah, I am putting myself, my sword and whoever is with me at your service and at the service of your religion." Then he bade farewell to Rasulullah ﷺ and the Muslims and left to fulfill his intention.

When he reached the valley of Makkah, he began shouting with his great resonant voice the

Talbiyyah, as taught by Rasulullah ﷺ: *"Labbaik Allahumma labbaik...* Here I am at your command, O Allah. Here I am; no partner have You. Here I am. Praise, blessings and all power on earth belong to You. No partner have You."

Thus, Thumamah ﷺ was the first Muslim on earth who ever entered Makkah making the *Talbiyyah*.

The Quraish heard the sound of the *Talbiyyah* and stopped what they were doing. They were both angry and alarmed. Holding their swords, they went towards the voice, intending to punish whoever dared to challenge them. When the people reached him, Thumamah ﷺ raised his voice higher with the *Talbiyyah* and looked at them with pride.

A young man from the Quraish was about to shoot him with an arrow when the others grabbed his hand and said, "Curse you! Don't you know who he is? He is Thumamah ibn Athal, chief of Yamamah. By god, if you hurt him, his people will cut our supplies and starve to death!"

After placing their swords back into their scabbards, the people came to Thumamah ﷺ. They said, "What is wrong with you, Thumamah? Have you abandoned your religion, the religion of your forefathers?"

"Nothing is wrong with me!" replied

Thumamah ﷺ. "I have found the best religion, the religion of Muhammad ﷺ!" Then he added, "I swear to you by the Lord of the *Ka`bah*, that after my return to Yamamah, no grain of wheat or any of our other goods shall reach you before you all follow Muhammad ﷺ."

Thumamah ﷺ performed *Umrah* under the watchful eyes of the Quraish, just as Rasulullah ﷺ had instructed him. He made sacrifice, dedicating it to Allah ﷻ, not to the idols. When Thumamah ﷺ returned home, he ordered his people to keep all supplies from the Quraish. They obeyed, and kept all their goods from the people of Makkah.

This boycott gradually began to hurt the Quraish. They started having severe food shortages. Hunger became so intense that some of the Quraish feared they would die. They finally had no choice but to write to the Prophet ﷺ, saying, "You had always been well-known for maintaining the bonds of kinship and urging others to do so. Now you have cut the bonds of kinship: you have killed the fathers with swords and let the sons die from hunger. Thumamah ibn Athal has kept all provisions from us. He has hurt us. Cannot grain be supplied from Yamamah?"

These were the same Quraish who had tortured, beaten and tried to starve the Muslims. They were the same ones who had tried to kill

Rasulullah ﷺ and his companions. And Rasulullah ﷺ had not stopped the grain or asked Thumamah ؓ to stop it; Thumamah ؓ had done that all on his own. The Prophet ﷺ could easily have left the boycott in place and taken revenge on the Makkans. But that was not his nature, for Allah ﷻ had created him different from other humans; he was the most merciful of all creation.

Rasulullah ﷺ wrote to Thumamah ؓ telling him to resume trade with Makkah, and Thumamah ؓ immediately restored supplies to their usual amount.

May Allah ﷻ raise Thumamah ؓ in Jannah and reward him for his support of the Prophet ﷺ.

142

Tufail ibn 'Amr ad-Dawsi

"O Allah, give him a sign."
Muhammad Rasulullah ﷺ

ufail ibn 'Amr ad-Dawsi was the chief of the Daws tribe. He was known for his hospitality; Tufail would have food served to anyone who visited his home, and his door was open to everyone. He always fed the hungry, comforted the frightened, and protected whomever sought protection. He was known to be a very kind and generous man.

Tufail was also a very sensitive poet. He had a keen sense for the Arabic language and words, and could feel deeply what a writer was trying to convey, whether it was a good expression or a bitter one. Therefore, the spoken word had a powerful influence on him.

Tufail left his home in Tihamah to travel to Makkah. At the time he was traveling, the struggle between the Prophet ﷺ and the unbelievers of Quraish had already begun. Both parties were trying to gain more allies. Rasulullah ﷺ was preaching for Allah ﷻ, and his weapons were the Truth and the Holy Qur'an. The unbelievers were resisting by all means, and using every weapon from words to swords to fire.

Tufail found himself caught in the middle of this struggle. He had not intended to get involved in any kind of conflict when he left for Makkah. Tufail was not even aware of the friction between Rasulullah ﷺ and the Quraish, but soon his interactions with the two sides would prove to be very significant. He would be affected by the conflict so much that his life would be changed forever.

Tufail related the story of how the conflict affected him:

> As soon as I came to Makkah, I was generously received by the chiefs of Quraish, and was extravagantly honored by them. Soon after my arrival, they all came to me together and said, "Tufail, you are a visitor to our city so let us give you our news. A man named Muhammad ibn 'Abdullah has been pretending

to be a prophet of Allah. He has left from under our authority and is trying to split our community. We are afraid he will do to you and to the chiefs of your tribe what he has done to us. If you run into him while you are here, don't talk to him, and don't listen to anything he has to say, because when he speaks he is like a sorcerer."

By Allah, they went on telling me about his "sorcery," scaring me so much that I decided not to approach that man, or talk to him, or listen to him.

The next morning I went to make *Tawaf* around the *Ka'bah*, to glorify the idols we used to worship. I put cotton in my ears so that not a word of Muhammad's teachings would reach my hearing.

But as soon as I got into the sacred area I found the Prophet ﷺ standing in front of the *Ka'bah*, making a prayer that didn't look like the ways of our traditions. I was much taken by this scene. I found myself walking nearer and nearer to him until I was quite close to him, despite my will. It was the will of Allah that I should hear some of what he was saying - it was so beautiful that I told myself, "Woe to you, Tufail! You are an intelligent poet; you are able to differentiate the good from the bad. Why don't you listen to the man? If what he says is good, accept it, and if it's bad, reject it!'

I stood there until the Prophet ﷺ left for his house. I followed him. When he entered the house, I followed him in and said, "Muhammad, your people told me many bad things about you. They scared me so much that I put cotton in my ears to prevent myself from hearing you. But the will of Allah let me hear your speech and I found it good. So please explain to me what this is all about."

He explained it to me and read *Surah al-Ikhlas* and *Surah al-Falaq*. I swear, I've never heard anything better than that nor have I met someone more fair on this earth. On the spot, I gave him my hand and pronounced the *Shahadah* that there is no god but Allah and that Muhammad is His messenger, and I became a Muslim.

I stayed in Makkah for a while to learn the teachings of Islam and to memorize what I could of the Qur'an. When I decided to go back to my people, I said, "O Messenger of Allah, I have influence upon my people. I am going back to them and I shall invite them to Islam. Pray to Allah that He gives me a sign to help me in inviting them." So he ﷺ prayed, "O Allah, give him a sign." So, I went back to my people.

When I was about to reach my land, I felt a light falling between my eyes just like a lamp. I said, "O Allah, put it somewhere else but not my face, for I am afraid my tribe might think it is a penalty for leaving their religion." So the light moved to the tip of my whip, and it shone on the people as if it were a suspended lamp.

When I saw my elderly father, I said, "Don't approach me, Father. I am no longer from you, and you're not from me."

He said, "Why, son?"

I said, "I have become Muslim and I follow the religion of Muhammad ibn 'Abdullah of Makkah."

He said softly, "Son, your religion is my religion!"

Delighted at these words I said, "Go, wash yourself, put on clean clothes, then come to me so I may teach you what I have been taught!"

So he went and did so. Then he came back and I explained Islam to him and he became a Muslim.

Then my wife came, so I said, "Don't come to me, for I am no longer from you, and you are no longer from me."

She said, "By the gods, why so?"

I said, "Islam has separated us. I am a

Muslim now and I follow the religion of Muhammad ibn 'Abdullah of Makkah."

She likewise said, "Then your religion is my religion!"

I said, "Go, purify yourself with the waterfall near the idol of our god Dhu ash-Shara."

She said, "Do you fear something from the god Dhu ash-Shara?"

I said, "I fear neither you nor Dhu ash-Shara. I simply told you to go and wash yourself there because it is far away from the people. I promise you, that piece of rock won't do you any harm."

So she went, washed and came back. I explained Islam to her and she became Muslim.

Then I invited all of the Daws tribe to Islam but they reacted slowly. Only Abu Hurairah was quick to respond to the invitation.

I returned to Rasulullah ﷺ at Makkah, and Abu Hurairah was with me. Rasulullah ﷺ asked me, "What news do you bring, my Tufail?"

I said, "I left my people with covered hearts and firm disbelief. Sins and disobedience have won over the Banu Daws."

Rasulullah ﷺ stood up and made *Wudu'*, and raised his hands to the sky. Abu Hurairah said, "When I saw that, I was afraid that he would pray to destroy my people and they would be ruined, so I whispered, 'O, my people!'"

But Rasulullah ﷺ kept saying, *"O Allah, guide the Daws, guide the Daws, guide the Daws."* Then he turned to me and said, "Go back to your people, treat them gently, and invite them to Islam."

I stayed with the Daws inviting them to Islam until the Prophet's ﷺ immigration to Madinah. After the battles of Badr, 'Uhud and the Trench I came to Rasulullah ﷺ with eighty families from Daws who had entered Islam and become good Muslims.

The Prophet ﷺ was pleased with us and gave us a portion of the booty of the town of Khaibar. So we said: "O Messenger of Allah, make us the right wing of your army in every battle and accept our slogan, 'At Your Command.'"

I stayed with Rasulullah ﷺ until Allah gave him the conquest of Makkah, and I asked him then, "O Rasulullah, send me to Dhul Kaffain, the idol of the Daws, so that I may burn it."

Rasulullah ﷺ gave me permission, and I went to the idol with a group of my people. When I arrived there, intending to burn it, men, women and children gathered around me. They expected to see me struck by lightning when I tried to destroy Dhul Kaffain. But I went straight to the idol, right in front of its worshippers, and began putting fire around it, chanting,

O Dhul-Kaffain, we're not your worshippers. We were born long before you were. I am filling your heart with fire!

As the fire devoured the idol, it devoured the remaining *Shirk* of the tribe of Daws. The whole tribe observed the helplessness of their idol. They all embraced Islam together and they all became Muslims.

May Allah ﷻ reward Tufail ibn 'Amr ad-Dawsi for his efforts to spread the message of Islam.

'Uqbah ibn 'Amir al-Juhani

"Would you lose the companionship of the Prophet ﷺ for sheep?"
Uqbah ibn 'Amir al-Juhani ﷺ

The night was cold, as it always is in the deserts near Madinah. The dark sky was dotted with bright shining stars, hundreds and thousands of them. A deep silence stretched over the land, and not a sound could be heard except from the small group of men who were huddled near each other. They sat close together around a small fire, trying to keep warm, and their flock of sheep idled nearby.

They were a simple people, the men of this group, with hardly any belongings. Neither they nor their animals had enough to satisfy the hunger all of them were feeling. They sat together in a setting very familiar to them. For these men, it seemed as if life was going on as usual. And yet, there was change in the air, change which none of them had yet perceived. The *Hijrah* of Rasulullah ﷺ had just taken place, and their lives, and the lives of everyone around them, were about to change dramatically forever.

In Madinah, some distance away, there was great excitement and rejoicing. Rasulullah ﷺ had finally come, after suffering much hardship in his city of Makkah. The Muslims of Madinah had much hope in the coming of the Prophet ﷺ. They themselves had been torn with division and feuding. They hoped that the presence of Rasulullah ﷺ was the blessing they needed to save themselves and their city from more trouble.

They would indeed find that his presence would better their situation tremendously, but it was not to be a quick cure. Rasulullah ﷺ, through his patient teaching and counsel, would bring out the best in them, so that they would become models for the rest of humankind.

Divine light had arrived in Madinah, in the being of Rasulullah ﷺ, and the entire city would be changed. Even its name would be changed, from the old Yathrib to *Madinah al-Munawwarah*, "the Radiant City."

The City of Light

The radiance and excitement of Madinah reached out to touch the hearts of whomever Allah ﷻ so desired. Soon it reached the simple shepherds of the deserts. The excitement was contagious, and before long, the shepherds themselves were longing to meet the Prophet ﷺ. They also hoped that Rasulullah ﷺ would make a difference in their lives, and help fill a void that was present in their hearts.

'Uqbah ibn 'Amir al-Juhani ﷺ was one of these shepherds. Later in life, after he had been touched by the Light of Rasulullah ﷺ, he would become a very learned man and a great collector of *ahadith*. 'Uqbah ﷺ left us his own words about how he came to be affected by Rasulullah ﷺ:

> The Prophet ﷺ came to al-Madinah while I was tending my sheep. As soon as I heard the news, I left my sheep and went to him, for nothing would have stopped me. When I met him, I said, "Would you take from me my *Bay'ah*, my pledge of loyalty?"
>
> "Who are you?" he asked.
>
> I said, "I am 'Uqbah ibn 'Amir al-Juhani."
>
> "Which would you prefer," he asked, "the oath of the Arabs of the desert or the oath of *Hijrah?*"

I said, "The oath of *Hijrah*." So Rasulullah
🕊 gave me the oath he gave to the *Muhajirun*. I
spent one night with him, then went back to my
sheep.

We were a group of twelve shepherds
who became Muslims and we lived far from
Madinah tending our sheep in the desert.

We said to each other, "There will be no
good in us if we don't go to Rasulullah 🕊, day
after day, so that he can teach us our religion
and allow us to hear the revelation that descends
on him from the Heavens. Every day we should
send one of us to Madinah, leaving his sheep to
the others to tend."

"Go," I said, "go to Rasulullah 🕊 one
after the other and leave your sheep to me," for
I was concerned about my little sheep.

My friends kept going to Rasulullah 🕊,
one after the other, each one leaving his sheep
to me. When each came back, I listened to what
he heard and I learned from him what he had
been taught. But soon I thought, "Woe to me!
Would you lose the companionship of the
Prophet 🕊 for sheep?" So I left my sheep and
went to Madinah to live in the *Masjid* near
Rasulullah 🕊.

Changes to Come

When he made this decision to live near Rasulullah ﷺ, 'Uqbah ؓ surely could not have imagined what this meant for his future. There was no way he could have known that within ten years, his mind and heart would be completely transformed through the blessed company of Rasulullah ﷺ. 'Uqbah ؓ would become one of the greatest thinkers and one of the most accomplished reciters of the Qur'an.

He would also become a notable military leader and would be one of those who conquered Damascus with Khalid ibn al-Walid ؓ. When making his decision to leave his sheep, there was no way 'Uqbah ؓ could know that one day, he would have a house in the green gardens of Damascus or that he would also have a house near the mighty Nile.

All these coming changes were hidden from the humble shepherd. 'Uqbah ؓ simply took the first step toward Allah ﷻ and His Prophet ﷺ. This first step of faith enabled him to give up all the attachments of the world and go, empty-handed, into a new life, not knowing what would happen next.

May Allah ﷻ bless 'Uqbah ibn Amir al-Juhani ؓ,
the man of knowledge and Jihad.

156

Wahshi ibn Harb

"I killed the best of people after the Prophet and I also killed the worst."
Wahshi ibn Harb 🕮

ahshi ibn Harb al-Habashi 🕮, nicknamed Abu Dasamah, was an Ethiopian. He was brought up as a slave and trained as a spearsman. He was very accomplished in this, for his spear never missed its mark. His skill was often used by other people to their advantage. During his lifetime, Wahshi killed one of the greatest and most beloved of the Muslims. Later on, he also killed a man who was destroying the faith of many Muslims. But the circumstances surrounding each murder were vastly different.

Wahshi's story is a severe one. He has told most of it himself:

> I was a fragile little boy, owned by Jubair ibn Mutkim, one of the chiefs of Quraish. Jubair's uncle Tukaimah was killed in the Battle of Badr by Hamzah, the Prophet's ﷺ uncle. Jubair felt so angry that he swore by the idols Lat and 'Uzza to take revenge. So he kept waiting for the proper opportunity to get even with Hamzah.
>
> Not long after Badr, the Quraish planned to go out to 'Uhud to wipe out the Muslims once and for all and to get revenge for relatives killed at Badr. They mobilized their troops and gathered their allies. When they were ready, they assigned the chief Abu Sufyan ibn Harb to be their leader.
>
> Abu Sufyan decided to take along with the army some of the women whose fathers, brothers or sons were killed at the Battle of Badr. He brought them to feed the army's enthusiasm for fighting and to prevent the men from running away, for they would be ashamed to leave the women.
>
> Among these women was his own wife Hind bint 'Utbah. Her father, her uncle and her

brother were all killed at Badr, so she was very thirsty for revenge.

When the Makkan army was about to leave, my master, Jubair ibn Mutkim, turned to me and said, "Would you like to free yourself from slavery, Wahshi?"

"Who would give that freedom to me?" I replied. "I would," he said. "If you kill Hamzah, the uncle of Muhammad, in revenge for my uncle Tukaimah, you're free."

"Who will guarantee that you keep this promise?" I asked. "Whoever you want," he replied, "and I'll make all the people witnesses."

"Sure, I'll do it! I'm trained for this," I said. I am an Ethiopian man and with the spear I never miss my target when I throw.

I took my spear and went with the army. I stayed in the back ranks with the women, for I had no interest in general fighting, only to earn my freedom.

When we reached the plain of 'Uhud and met the army of Islam, I went looking for Hamzah. I knew him from before, as he was known to everybody. He used to put an ostrich feather in his turban when he fought, so he could be recognized. This was a practice of all the courageous Arab fighters.

Finally, I found my opportunity and

killed Hamzah ﷺ with one throw of my spear. After the battle, the women of Quraish were jubilant that revenge had been exacted for their family members killed at Badr. Hind was so happy on seeing Hamzah ﷺ dead, she gave me her gold necklace and earrings, saying, "They are all yours, Wahshi, all yours...keep them, they are valuable!"

When the battle of 'Uhud was over, I went back to Makkah with the army. Jubair, my master, fulfilled his promise and set me free.

But the influence of Muhammad ﷺ kept growing and the number of Muslims kept increasing day after day. As this matter grew greater and greater, my grief and fear grew greater and greater as well, until I could not think about anything else. I remained in that state until Muhammad ﷺ conquered Makkah with his enormous army.

Then I ran away to the town of Ta'if, seeking security. But soon after that, the people of Ta'if turned to Islam, and they appointed a delegation to meet Muhammad ﷺ and declare their entrance into his religion.

I was driven to despair; I didn't know where to go. I thought about fleeing to Syria, Yemen or any other land. I was completely absorbed by my grief, when a man advised me,

"Woe to you, Wahshi. By Allah, Muhammad does not kill a man who enters into his religion."

As soon as I heard these words, I left for Madinah to meet the Prophet ﷺ. When I got there, I looked for him and found him in the *Masjid an-Nabawi*. I worked my way through the crowd cautiously until I stood by his head and then I said, "I testify that there is no diety but Allah and that Muhammad is His Messenger."

When he heard these words, he looked up at me and then turned his eyes away from me and said, "You are Wahshi, are you not?"

"Yes, Rasulullah," I replied.

The Prophet ﷺ said, "Sit down and tell me how you killed my uncle Hamzah."

I sat down and told him the story. When my speech was over, he turned away from me and said, "Your Islam is accepted Wahshi, but go away from me. I don't want to look upon you again."

From that day, I tried to avoid him, not wanting to upset him. When the companions sat in front of him, I used to take a place well behind them. I kept doing this until the Prophet ﷺ was taken to his Lord.

In spite of knowing that Islam erases what happened before, I remained conscious of the severity of what I'd done. I kept waiting for the chance when I might make up for my sins.

When the Prophet ﷺ died and Abu Bakr took over the leadership, the Banu Hanifah tribe of the Najd abandoned Islam and followed Musailimah the Liar. Abu Bakr mobilized an army to fight and bring the Banu Hanifah back to the religion of Allah.

I told myself, "By Allah, this is your chance. Take it; don't let it go."

I went with the Muslim army, taking with me the same spear with which I had killed Hamzah ibn 'Abd al-Muttalib ﷺ. I committed myself either to kill Musailimah with that spear or to die trying, obtaining *Shahadah*.

On the day of the Battle of Yamamah, I was with the Muslims when they broke into the "Garden of Death," where Musailimah and his followers were taking refuge and where a great number of them were killed. As our army met with the enemy, I kept watching Musailimah. He was standing with his sword in his hand and I saw that a man from *Ansar* was watching him as well. We both wanted to kill him. In the end, we both attacked him at the same time, and only Allah knows which one of us actually killed him.

May Allah ﷻ accept the repentance of Wahshi ﷺ and reward him for his sincere efforts to make up for his past. Amin.

Zaman ibn Salabah

"If this person of braids has spoken the truth, he will surely enter the Garden."
Muhammad Rasulullah ﷺ

The story of Zaman ibn Salabah ◌ is yet another short example of the remarkable personalities of the companions of Rasulullah ﷺ. This *Sahabi* was not a distinguished Makkan; he did not die a martyr in battle; and he was not a great scholar. However, he effectively opened the door for countless people to become Muslim. How did he do it? By being truthful and by asking the right questions - just by being himself.

There are some people who never ask questions because they always want others to think they are very intelligent. Others, because they are too shy, will never ask questions for fear of embarrassment. But Zaman ﷺ was not like the people of either of these two groups. When he had a question in his mind, he just went ahead and asked. Rasulullah ﷺ loved truthfulness and he sensed the sincerity of Zaman ﷺ. So the Prophet ﷺ answered in a clear, concise and truthful manner, and the answers he gave Zaman ﷺ have been useful to Muslims ever since.

The Inquisitive Visitor

One day Rasulullah ﷺ and some of the *Sahabah* were sitting in the *Masjid an-Nabawi* in Madinah. It was in the ninth year after the *Hijrah*. Many people were coming from all over Arabia to learn about Islam and to meet the Prophet ﷺ who had so much power over minds and hearts. Some came because they were curious, and others came because they thought it would be wise to make friends with this powerful man. Still, there were those who came because they sensed that he was the true prophet of Allah ﷻ.

At this time, a nomad from the desert arrived at the *Masjid* and, in the proud manner of his people, pushed his way past everyone and called out in a loud voice, "Where is the son of the Bani Hashim?"

164

"I am the son of Bani Hashim," answered the Prophet ﷺ. "What do you want?"

"Is your name Muhammad?"

"Yes it is," replied the Messenger ﷺ.

"Look. I'm from the desert. I am not an educated man. But I want to ask you some questions. Will you resent the rough manner of my speech?"

"Never! You may ask whatever you want. I shall not mind."

The *Sahabah*, including 'Umar, Talhah, and Anas ﷺ were somewhat tense. They were always cautious when strangers approached Rasulullah ﷺ in a rough manner.

They all began to listen.

This nomad was a young man. He was handsome, tall, with dark olive skin and black hair that was long and set in braids that fell down his back, which is the fashion of some nomadic Arabs to this day.

The bedouin tribes spoke very pure Arabic. The children of city folk, including the Prophet ﷺ himself, were often sent to the nomads in their early years to learn the purer form of Arabic. So although Zaman ﷺ apologized for his rough speech, he actually proceeded to ask his questions in a very beautiful way. He spoke so well that 'Umar ﷺ later said, "I have never come across anyone who spoke as eloquently as Zaman."

Zaman began: "O Muhammad! Your preacher came to our tribe and explained that you are convinced that Allah has raised you to be His Messenger."

"Yes, he was correct in his statement."

"Who created the heavens?"

"Allah," said Rasulullah ﷺ.

"Who created the earth?" asked the bedouin.

"Allah," answered Rasulullah ﷺ.

"Who set down the mountains and who created the variety of things on them? Has Allah actually sent you down as His Messenger?"

"Yes," was the Prophet's ﷺ simple reply.

"Your preacher said that we have to perform five daily prayers."

"He spoke the truth."

"In the Name of the Supreme Being Who conferred prophethood upon you, has He really commanded performance of the prayers?"

"Yes," said the Prophet ﷺ.

"Your preacher also said that we must pay the *Zakah* from our wealth, once a year."

"He spoke the truth," said Rasulullah ﷺ.

"In the Name of the Supreme Being Who conferred prophethood upon you, has He really commanded this payment?"

"Yes."

"Your preacher told us to observe fast every year, during the entire month of Ramadan."

"Yes, he spoke the truth," replied the Prophet 爨.

"In the Name of Allah Who has sent you as a messenger, has He Himself ordered this?"

"Yes."

"Your preacher also said that a pilgrimage to the House of Allah is required for one who can afford it."

"He spoke the truth."

The bedouin had finished with his questions. He gave the *Shahadah* and then said, "O Messenger of Allah! My community has chosen me to visit you as its messenger. My name is Zaman ibn Salabah and I am a member of the Banu Sa`d. I swear in the name of the Supreme Being Who has appointed you as a true prophet that I shall neither add to nor omit anything from what you have told me."

After saying this, he greeted the group of *Sahabah* respectfully and then went home. The Prophet 爨 watched him leave and said, "If this person with braids has spoken the truth, he will surely enter Heaven."

Now, Zaman's 爨 tribe was the Banu Sa`d. The preacher who came to them was from among the group of *Sahabah* that Rasulullah 爨 had sent all over Arabia. These preachers were sent to different places after the Treaty of Hudaibiyyah made it possible for Muslims to move about safely. The tribe listened to the preacher, but thought it best to send one of its respected members to visit the Prophet ﷺ personally. That is why Zaman ﷺ had come.

Taking the Message Home

When he got back to his tribe, all the people assembled around him to find out what he had seen and done and learned in Makkah. After the first greetings had been exchanged, everyone settled down to listen. Zaman ﷺ was a man without doubts. He said right off, "Down with the idols Lat and 'Uzza! They are wretched and disgraced!"

His people were outraged and horrified. They thought that if one spoke disrespectfully about the idols, one would meet some terrible disaster and even the whole tribe might be ruined. So they shouted at Zaman ﷺ and told him to stop and repent.

Zaman ﷺ, however, had just become a Muslim. He was completely sure and certain of his new faith. After all, he had just returned from a meeting with the Prophet ﷺ, and the light of this meeting was still on him. So he addressed his people with sincere conviction:

"O people of my tribe! Listen to me carefully. Lat and 'Uzza are mere lumps of stone and wood. They neither benefit nor harm anyone. How sad it is that you take them as objects of worship. Only Allah ﷻ deserves to be worshipped. The Supreme Lord is One. He has sent down Muhammad ﷺ as His Messenger and revealed to him His Book, which is the fountain and source of guidance and welfare. Practicing the teachings of this Book, you will come out of the swamp of error into which you have been sunk up to your necks. I have found the Truth. I bear witness that there is no deity except Allah ﷻ and that Muhammad ﷺ is His servant and messenger. Obey me and believe in Allah ﷻ and His Prophet ﷺ. In that lies your welfare, otherwise you will be ruined. I have learned all the things which you must do and all the things from which you must abstain."

The truly amazing thing was what followed. Zaman's ﷺ speech was so effective, that the people of Banu Sa'd were able to actually hear and understand the truth of what he was saying. Perhaps all of them knew how to sincerely ask real questions. Perhaps all of them were fed up with the idols and knew in their hearts, as all people really do, that Allah ﷻ is the source of all benefit and goodness. In any case, by nightfall, every single member of that tribe had become Muslim.

The great scholar and *Sahabi* 'Abdullah ibn Abbas ﷺ said that he never saw a community better than that of Zaman ﷺ.

May Allah ﷻ bless him and be pleased with Zaman for his sincere belief and his great service to his people.

Zaid al-Khair

"You have two characteristics that Allah and His Prophet like: forbearance and patience."
Muhammad Rasulullah 鷺

asulullah 鷺 was an extraordinary human being, the best of all creation. The beauty and power that he possessed were witnessed by the *Sahabah* who were with him. Their stories of how their hearts were changed profoundly, sometimes just through one meeting with him, show how truly remarkable he was.

The people who saw the Truth in his message were remarkable people as well. Some of them were the best of people before Islam, during the days of *Jahiliyyah*, the days of Ignorance. And these were the same people who were the best of the Muslims after they had accepted Islam. Their actions and even their instincts before accepting

171

Islam were already righteous and good. So when they came across the message of Islam, it seemed to fit their existing characters perfectly. The story of Zaid al-Khair ﷺ is one example of such an exceptional person. Though he was only in the company of Rasulullah ﷺ for a few days, he is one who will forever be remembered as an amazing *Sahabi*.

The Generous Warrior

"Zaid al-Khail," or "Zaid of the horses" was what this *Sahabi* was known as in the days of *Jahiliyyah*. He was very well known among the Arabs. Not only was he well-respected because he was the chief of his people and a fearsome warrior, but he was also known for his generosity and hospitality.

There is a famous story of Zaid ﷺ before he had become Muslim, which illustrates how truly generous he was. In this story, Zaid gives a large number of camels to a poor man, who earlier had tried to steal a herd from Zaid and his blind father. Zaid even sent some of his men to protect the poor man until he reached his children with his new wealth.

Meeting the Prophet ﷺ

Some time later, the news of the Prophet ﷺ reached Zaid al-Khail. He also heard about some of what Rasulullah ﷺ was teaching, and so he began preparing himself for a trip to Madinah. He also invited a delegation of his people to accompany him, so that they could all go and meet this prophet who was teaching such moral and upright behavior.

Zaid left for Madinah with a big delegation from Tayyi. They rode a long way across the desert, and at last they reached Madinah. They headed directly to the Prophet's ﷺ *Masjid* and knelt their camels down at its door.

It happened that, as they entered, Rasulullah ﷺ was on his *Minbar* giving a speech to the Muslims. The visitors were moved by his words, and they were also amazed to see how attentive and respectful the Muslims were to him and to everything he said. They sat down quietly at the back of the *Masjid* and listened.

When Rasulullah ﷺ saw them, he addressed himself to the Muslims, as if he didn't know the others were there, inviting them to worship Allah ﷻ and to leave the worship of idols.

The delegation had two different reactions to the words of the Prophet ﷺ. Most of them accepted the truth with enthusiasm. One rejected it and headed for *ash-Sham* (present-day Syria), where he shaved his head like a monk and became a Christian.

The reaction of Zaid and others was different. As soon as Rasulullah ﷺ had finished his speech, Zaid stood up in the midst of the Muslims. He was such a big man that his feet reached the earth while he was riding his horse as if he were riding a donkey. So in the *Masjid* he towered over most of the people, and he said in a loud, clear voice, "O Muhammad, I testify that there is no god but Allah and that you are the messenger of Allah!"

The Prophet ﷺ came right over to him and asked him who he was.

"I am Zaid al-Khail ibn Muhalhil."

Rasulullah ﷺ said, "Thank Allah Who brought you from your valley and your mountains and softened your heart towards Islam."

Then Rasulullah ﷺ took him to his house. With them were 'Umar ibn al-Khattab ﷺ and some other companions. At home, the Prophet ﷺ gave him a mat, but Zaid ﷺ was ashamed to recline in the presence of the Prophet ﷺ and gave the mat back to him. The Prophet ﷺ gave it to him again. Zaid ﷺ gave it back. He gave it again, and again Zaid ﷺ returned it. Both Rasulullah ﷺ and Zaid ﷺ were incredibly polite.

When they were all seated, Rasulullah ﷺ said to Zaid ﷺ, "No Arab has ever been spoken of in the highest terms except that he falls below what was said of him. The only exception is Zaid al-Khail; he exceeds all that has been said about him." Then he added, "O Zaid, you have two characteristics that Allah and His Prophet like."

Zaid ﷺ said, "And what are those, O Rasulullah ﷺ?"

"Self-control and patience."

Zaid ﷺ replied, "Thank Allah Who has given me what He and His Prophet ﷺ like!" Then he turned to the Prophet ﷺ and said, "Give me, O Rasulullah, three hundred horsemen and I guarantee you that we will conquer the territory of Byzantium!"

"What a man you are, Zaid!" said the Prophet ﷺ, who liked enthusiasm. He changed his visitor's name from al-Khail (the Horse) to al-Khair (the Good). Thereafter he was known as Zaid al-Khair, or Zaid the Good.

An Unfortunate Illness

When Zaid ﷺ at last prepared to return home to the Najd, Rasulullah ﷺ said farewell to him and told his companions, "What a great man he will be, if he is to be saved from the fever of

Madinah." At that time there was an epidemic of fever in the city, and many newcomers caught it who were not used to the air of the place. Indeed, soon after Zaid ﷺ left Madinah he fell ill with that fever. He said to those who were with him, "Don't stop here. Take me away from the land of Qais. We used to be enemies in the *Jahiliyyah*. They are Muslim now but will not know that I am. By Allah, I will never fight a Muslim until I meet Allah."

Zaid ﷺ kept going on his way home to the Najd in spite of his fever. He hoped to reach his people and to make them Muslims, with the grace of Allah ﷺ. He struggled to overcome the fever but could not, and he died while they were camped at the oasis of Farda in the Najd. Between his entrance into Islam and his death, there was hardly any time to fall into sin.

May Allah ﷺ bless him and be pleased
with him and grant him
His generosity as he was generous
to the creation
of Allah ﷺ on
earth.

Appendix

Transliterated Names of the Sahabah ﷺ and Other Historical Notables

'Abdullah ibn 'Abbās

'Abdullah ibn 'Amr

Abu Bakr as-Ṣiddīq

Abu Hurairah ad-Dawsī al-Yamānī

Abu Sufyān ibn Ḥarb

Abu Sufyān ibn al-Ḥārith

'Ādi ibn Ḥātim aṭ-Ṭā'ī

'Ā'ishah bint Abi Bakr

'Alā' ibn Ḥadhramī

'Alī ibn Abi Ṭālib

'Āmir ibn Juwain

'Ammār ibn 'Abasah

'Ammār ibn Yāsir

'Amr ibn al-Jamūh

al-Arqam ibn Abi al-Arqam

'Āṣim ibn 'Umar ibn al-Khaṭṭāb

'Ayyāsh ibn Abi Rabī'ah

Bilāl ibn Rabāh

Dirār ibn al-Azwar

Halīmah as-Saʿdiyyah

Ḥamzah ibn ʿAbdul Muṭṭalib

Ḥārith ibn Ḥishām

Ḥatim aṭ-Ṭāʾī

Hind bint ʿAmr

Hind bint ʿUtbah

ʿIkrimah ibn Abi Jahl

Jaʿfar ibn Abi Sufyān ibn al-Ḥārith

Khālid ibn al-Walīd

Khallād ibn ʿAmr

Mālik ibn Jubair

Marwān ibn al-Ḥakam

Muʿādh ibn ʿAmr

Muʿādh ibn Jabal

Muʿāwiyah ibn Abi Sufyan

Muʿawwadh ibn ʿAmr

Muṣʿab ibn ʿUmair

Nuʿaim ibn Masʿūd

Nuʿaimān an-Najjārī

Nuʾmān ibn Muqarrin al-Muzanī

Sa'd ibn Abi Waqqāṣ

Salmān al-Fārisī

Sinān ibn Mālik an-Numairī

Ṣuhaib ibn Sīnān ar-Rumī

Surāqah ibn Mālik

Tha'labah ibn Mālik

Thumāmah ibn Āthal

Ṭufail ibn 'Amr ad-Dawsī

'Umar ibn 'Abdul 'Azīz

'Uqbah ibn 'Āmir al-Juhānī

'Uyainah ibn Ḥiln

Waḥshī ibn Ḥarb al-Ḥabashī

Zamān ibn Salabah

Zaid al-Khair

Zaid ibn Thābit

Zurrū ibn Sādūs

Glossary

adhān: the public call to prayer

amīr: leader

Amīr al-Mu'minīn: "Leader of the Believers"

Amīn: trustworthy

Anṣār: Helper; the Muslims native to Madinah who aided the Muslims of Makkah.

Bait al-Māl: the treasury

Bait al-Maqdis: "House of Holiness," Jerusalem

barakah: blessing

Bid'ah: innovation; change

bashārah: good news

bai'ah: pledge of allegiance

Bismika Allāhumma: "In your Name, O Allāh"

Bismillahi-ar-Rahmāni-ar-Rahīm: "In the name of Allah, the Merciful, the Compassionate."

Dār al-Hijrah: the place to which *hijrah* or immigration is made; refers to Madīnah.

da'wah: inviting others to embrace Islam by showing them the true *dīn* of Allāh ﷻ.

dīn: religion; way of life

dīnār: a unit of money worth 100 dirhams or about 53 dollars (US) *dirhams:* a unit of money worth about 50 cents (US)

du'ā': supplication

al-Fārūq: the one who distinguishes between right and wrong

Fāsiq: a sinner or wrongdoer

fatwā: religious ruling

fiqh: the details of Islamic jurisprudence

fitnah: mischief; calamity; chaos

Ḥadīth: the sayings of Rasulullah

Ḥajj: pilgrimage to Makkah during the first days of the month of *Dhu-(a)l Hijjah*

ḥalāl: lawful and pure

Alḥamdu-li-(A)llāh: "All Praises to Allāh"

ḥarām: forbidden; a protected place

Hijrah: the migration of Rasulullah from Makkah to Madinah. The Islamic calendar starts from this event.

hawdah: small room made to fit on a camel in which a woman could sit privately

ḥuffāẓ: those who memorized the Qur'an word for word (sing.: *ḥāfiẓ*)

'Īd: Islamic holiday

'ilm: knowledge

imām: the leader of the prayer or the community; also, a great religious scholar

182

īmān: faith

iqāmah: the second call to prayer

Jāhiliyyah: the days of ignorance before Islām

Jannah: Heaven; Paradise

Jannat al-Baqī': the privileged gravesite of companions.

jihād: struggle, both external and internal

al-Kāfirūn: the disbelievers (sing. *kāfir*)

al-Kawthar: the river of *Jannah*

khabbāb: older man

khair: blessings; goodness

Khalīfah: the successor of Rasulullah ﷺ; the leader of the Muslim community (pl. *khulafā'*)

khalīl: closest friend

Khulafā' ar-Rāshidūn: The rightly guided *khalīfahs.*

khuṭab: speeches, sermons (sing.: *khutbah*; *khatīb: n.* one who makes a speech or sermon)

kuffār: plural of *kāfir*; disbeliever; one who covers up the truth

Al-Madīnah al-Munawwarah: the City of Light

Maqām Ibrāhīm: The Station of Ibrāhīm

masjid: mosque

mahr: dower/wedding gift

Mi'rāj: Rasulullah's ﷺ night journey from Makkah
   to Jerusalem and to the Heavens

Muhājirūn: immigrants; those Muslims who
   migrated from Makkah to Madinah during the
   Hijrah

Mujāhidūn: those people who strive in the Way of
   Islam.

Munāfiqūn: hypocrites; those who pretend to
   believe, but who really don't.

mushaf: a written copy of the Holy Qur'ān

Mushrikūn: those who commit *shirk*; those who
   associate others with Allāh ﷻ; polytheists
   (sing.: *Mushrik*)

muwāfaqah: successful

Qārī: one who recites the holy Qur'an.

qiblah: the direction facing the Ka'bah in which
   Muslims pray.

al-Quds: Jerusalem

rak'ah: one section of the Muslim prayer that
   involves four positions: *Qiyām* (standing),
   Rukū' (bowing), *Qawmah* (second standing),
   and *Sajdah* (prostrating).

Ramaḍān: The month of fasting for Muslims in
   which the Qur'an was revealed to Prophet
   Muḥammad ﷺ

Rasūlullāh: The Messenger of Allāh ﷻ; Muḥammad
   son of Abdullāh ﷺ

aṣ-Ṣabirūn: the patient people

Ṣadaqah: charity

Ṣaḥābah: (sing: Ṣaḥābī) companions of Rasulullah ﷺ

As-Salsabīl: a spring in *Jannah*

As-Salāmu 'Alaikum: "Peace be with You;" the
    greeting of Islam.

Ṣalāh: the daily ritual prayers of Islam, done five
    times a day

Ṣalāt al-Fajr: one of the five ritual prayers
    performed at dawn

Ṣalāt al-Janāzah: Funeral prayer

shahādah: the profession of faith

shahīd: one who dies in the way of Allah ﷻ

Shaiṭān: Satan, the devil

Sharī'ah: the law; the perfected way for humans to
    live; the way of life given by Allāh ﷻ

shirk: to associate others with Allāh ﷻ

Subḥāna Allāh: "Glory Be to Allah"

suffah: porch or bench

Sunnah: the ways and instructions of Rasulullah ﷺ.

sūrah: a chapter of the Qur'ān

Tabi'ūn: those who were companions of the
    Sahabah ﷺ

taqwā: piety

Tarāwīḥ: special night prayer in Ramaḍān, either eight, ten, or twenty *Rak'āh*

ṭawwāf: circumambulation (usually in reference to the Ka'bah)

tayammum: ritual washing with clean earth, sand, or dust if water is not available

Uḥud: Site of one of the early battles in Islamic history.

Ummah: Muslim community

Ummahāt al-Mu'minīn: the Mothers of the Believers

Waḥī: revelation

wuḍū': ritual washing before prayer

zakāh: the purification of wealth; charity; alms

Islamic Invocations

Rasūlullāh, *Ṣalla Allahu ʿalaihi wa Sallam* (صَلَّى ٱللَّهُ عَلَيْهِ وَسَلَّم), and the Qurʾān teach us to glorify Allāh ﷻ when we mention His Name and to invoke His Blessings when we mention the names of His Angels, Messengers, the *Ṣaḥābah* and the Pious Ancestors.

When we mention the Name of Allāh we must say: *Subḥāna-hū Wa-Taʿālā* (سُبْحَانَهُ وَتَعَالَى), Glorified is He and High.

When we mention the name of Rasūlullāh ﷺ we must say: *Ṣalla Allāhu ʿalai-hi wa-Sallam,* (صَلَّى ٱللَّهُ عَلَيْهِ وَسَلَّم), May Allāh's Blessings and Peace be upon him.

When we mention the name of an angel or a prophet we must say: *Alai-hi-(a)s-Salām* (عَلَيْهِ ٱلسَّلَام), Upon him be peace.

When we hear the name of the *Ṣaḥābah* we must say:
For more than two, *Raḍiya-(A)llāhu Taʿālā ʿan-hum,* (رَضِيَ ٱللَّهُ تَعَالَى عَنْهُم), May Allāh be pleased with them.
For two of them, *Raḍiya-(A)llāhu Taʿālā ʿan-humā* (رَضِيَ ٱللَّهُ تَعَالَى عَنْهُمَا), May Allāh be pleased with both of them.
For a *Ṣaḥābī*, *Raḍiya-(A)llāhu Taʿālā ʿan-hu* (رَضِيَ ٱللَّهُ تَعَالَى عَنْهُ), May Allāh be pleased with him.
For a *Ṣaḥābiyyah*, *Raḍiya-(A)llāhu Taʿālā ʿan-hā* (رَضِيَ ٱللَّهُ تَعَالَى عَنْهَا), May Allāh be pleased with her.

When we hear the name of the Pious Ancestor *(As-Salaf as-Ṣāliḥ)* we must say
For a man, *Raḥmatu-(A)llāh ʿalai-hi* (رَحْمَةُ ٱللَّهِ عَلَيْهِ), May Allāh's Mercy be upon him.
For a woman, *Raḥmatu-(A)llāh ʿalai-hā* (رَحْمَةُ ٱللَّهِ عَلَيْهَا), May Allāh's Mercy be with her.

IQRA' Transliteration Chart

q	ق	z	ز	,	أ *
k	ك	s	س	b	ب
l	ل	sh	ش	t	ت
m	م	ṣ ص *		th	ث *
n	ن	ḍ ض *		j	ج
h	ه	ṭ ط *		ḥ	ح *
w	و	ẓ ظ *		kh	خ *
y	ي	' ع *		d	د
		gh غ *		dh	ذ *
		f	ف	r	ر

SHORT VOWELS	LONG VOWELS	DIPHTHONGS
a \ ﹷ	a \ ـَا	aw \ ـَوْ
u \ ﹹ	u \ ـُو	ai \ ـَيْ
i \ ﹻ	i \ ـِي	

Such as: *kataba* كَتَبَ	Such as: *Kitab* كِتَاب	Such as: *Lawḥ* لَوْح
Such as: *Qul* قُلْ	Such as: *Mamnun* مَمْنُون	Such as: *'Ain* عَيْن
Such as: *Ni'mah* نِعْمَة	Such as: *Dīn* دِين	

* Special attention should be given to the symbols marked with stars for they have no equivalent in the English sounds .